SOUPS

SOUPS

Over 200 of the best recipes

hamlyn

First published in Great Britain in 2007 by
Hamlyn, a division of Octopus Publishing Group Ltd,
2–4 Heron Quays, London E14 4JP

ISBN-13: 978-0-600-61144-8
ISBN-10: 0-600-61144-2

A CIP catalogue record for this book is available
from the British Library

Printed and bound in China

10 9 8 7 6 5 4 3 2 1

Notes

This book includes dishes made with nuts and nut derivatives. It is advisable for those with known allergic
reactions to nuts and nut derivatives and those who may be potentially vulnerable to these allergies, such as
pregnant and nursing mothers, invalids, the elderly, babies and children, to avoid dishes made with nuts
and nut oils. It is also prudent to check the labels of preprepared ingredients for the possible inclusion of
nut derivatives.

The Department of Health advises that eggs should not be consumed raw. This book contains some dishes
made with raw or lightly cooked eggs. It is prudent for more vulnerable people such as pregnant and
nursing mothers, invalids, the elderly, babies and young children to avoid uncooked or lightly cooked
dishes made with eggs.

Meat and poultry should be cooked thoroughly. To test if poultry is cooked, pierce the flesh through the
thickest part with a skewer or fork – the juices should run clear, never pink or red.

Both metric and imperial measurements are given for the recipes. Use one set of measures only, not a
mixture of both.

Ovens should be preheated to the specified temperature. If using a fan-assisted oven, follow the
manufacturer's instructions for adjusting the time and temperature. Grills should also be preheated.

contents

introduction

When it comes to quick, convenient and nutritious meals, a bowl of soup and a fresh crusty roll are the perfect solution. From hearty winter soups to clear broths and refreshing, chilled gazpachos, soup is extremely versatile and can be enjoyed whenever you feel like a speedy snack or an easy lunch or evening meal.

A hot bowl of homemade soup is the ultimate comfort food, and it can be extremely quick to prepare. Simply make large batches of your favourite recipe and keep it in the refrigerator for a day or two, or freeze it for later use. This way you can still enjoy a delicious meal even when you're really short of time or are too tired to prepare a meal from scratch. Some freshly chopped herbs or a handful of grated cheese will add the perfect finishing touch.

Some ingredients naturally work well together, and soup is the ideal way to enjoy these special combinations. Each has a unique flavour when cooked separately, but when they are simmered together in one pan, they merge to produce a very different taste. **Chicken and Sweetcorn Soup** (see page 45), **Pea and Mint Soup** (see page 123), **New Potato, Coriander and Leek Soup** (see page 126) and **Melon and Parma Ham Soup** (see page 251) are just some of the recipes in this book that use ingredients that work well together. However, you will also discover more unusual partners that result in surprising, but equally enjoyable, soups. **Spicy Apple and Potato Soup** (see page 128) and **Garlic and Almond Soup** (see page 224) are just a couple of examples.

In the following chapters you will find more than 200 soup recipes for every occasion and to suit every palate. Whether you have minutes or hours to create your soup, you will be spoilt for choice, and there are plenty of ideas for impressive dinner party starters as well as quick lunches. You will also find tips on preparing garnishes, a checklist of the equipment you will need and recipes for the basic stocks that are used in many of the soups in this book.

Soup through the ages

Soup was probably a regular fixture on the dinner menu as soon as ancient people had learned how to make fire and fashion a vessel in which to contain liquid. Many foods, including a large number of seeds and plants, are inedible unless they have been boiled, and this cooking method would have provided people with a more plentiful and varied diet. Although the cooking liquid may well have been secondary to the actual food in the pot, it would have represented a warming and nutritious drink. Over time, as an understanding of the ingredients developed, it was realized that otherwise bland – but nutritious – foods could be combined with more flavoursome ingredients to create interesting meals.

During the Middle Ages, soup was a popular dish, and the introduction of new and unusual ingredients from further afield led to the development of a good variety of vegetable and meat broths and soups. Soup could be prepared in advance and left to its own devices while the cook of the household got on with other courses.

Originally, soup would have been poured over bread before being eaten, and this is one of the theories about the origin of the word 'soup', because the drenched bread was referred to as 'sop'.

Eventually, however, soup began to be appreciated as a dish in its own right and was consumed directly from the bowl. As spoons were a relatively late addition to the dining table, this would have involved drinking it. The large bowl of soup would be passed around, with each person taking a few sips and maybe helping themselves to a chunk of meat or whatever ingredients had been cooked in the simmering liquid.

Throughout history, soup has been regarded as a suitable food for invalids, presumably because a warm broth is easy to consume and digest, and the dish could easily be adjusted to include particularly health-promoting foods. Even today, a comforting bowl of hot chicken soup is a favourite treatment for sufferers from colds and flu, and it is the food we turn to when we are feeling low or in need of a lift.

Home comforts

There is something comforting about a big saucepan of homemade soup simmering away on the hob. Even if you aren't particularly confident in the kitchen, you will be able to create delicious, simple soups using fresh ingredients and enjoy the benefits of tucking into a homemade meal. Any produce you happen to have in your kitchen can generally be transformed into a tasty soup, and making a soup is a great way of using up odd vegetables or meat left over from the Sunday roast. The best thing about homemade soup is that you know exactly what's going into it, so you can keep it as wholesome as you like.

Although there are many great soup varieties available to buy these days, there isn't a lot of effort involved in making your own. You can pick your flavour, adding more or less of certain ingredients depending on what you have available, and one session in the kitchen could result in enough soup for weeks. Buy some freezer-proof cartons or use food bags to freeze individual portions, so you only have to defrost the amount you need.

You can choose your recipes to reflect seasonally available ingredients and enjoy soup all year round. Although we traditionally regard soup as a winter dish, light broths and chilled soups can make a refreshing meal for a warm summer's day. In fact, a whole chapter is devoted to chilled soups in the book, with delicious recipes, such as **Iced Tomato Soup with Salsa Verde** (see page 235) and **Chilled Watercress Soup** (see page 238), offering you the satisfaction of creating appetizing dishes using the best local produce.

A healthy option

As well as often being a quick and simple meal, soup can also be a healthy choice. We all know that we're supposed to eat at least five portions of fresh fruit and vegetables every day, but this isn't always easy. Busy lifestyles or long hours in the office often mean that our diet suffers, and it's easy to resort to unhealthy snacks and ready-prepared meals when we're stressed or don't have much time to cook. Many of the recipes in this book include a varied selection of vegetables as well as fresh herbs, fragrant spices, pulses, seafood and poultry. A bowl of soup can be a well-balanced meal, and in addition you have the enjoyment of tucking into a homemade dish, which will always taste better than something from a packet or can.

The cooking techniques used to make soup mean that more of the valuable nutrients remain in the finished dish. Soup is often a one-pot meal with vegetables cooked in the stock, rather than in a separate pan, from which the cooking water – along with many of the vitamins – is discarded when the vegetables are boiled and strained. In most soup recipes, raw vegetables will simply be added to the stock or cooked in a little oil before the liquid is added. This is also a great way to cook pulses, and you'll find lentils, peas and beans in many recipes. Pulses are a rich source of protein and fibre, so they are a good choice for vegetarians and also a nutritious way of bulking up soup to make a more filling meal. Some dried pulses need presoaking, but others can be added directly to the soup, absorbing the flavours from the stock.

back to basics

The great thing about making soup is that you don't really need to buy any specialist equipment. A well-stocked kitchen will already contain everything you need to make most of the recipes in this book, but here's a rundown of the basics so that you can make sure that you have the necessary items to hand.

Set of saucepans

If you cook regularly, you will already have a selection of good-quality saucepans. It's worth spending as much as you can afford because you will then get a product that should last you for years. You will need a large, heavy-based saucepan for the actual soup as well as a smaller one for heating stocks and cooking other ingredients. A small, nonstick frying pan will also come in useful.

Sharp knives

You will need a large knife for chopping vegetables and smaller knives for filleting, cutting up smaller vegetables and for dicing meat.

Ladle

You will need a ladle for serving the soup, whether you are transferring it from the saucepan direct to soup bowls or serving at the table where the soup is presented in a decorative tureen.

Blender or food processor

Many soups are partly blended, and sometimes the whole soup is blended, so a blender or food processor will prove useful if you're planning to make lots of soup. A food processor is also useful as a quick, effortless way of chopping onions and other vegetables. If you don't have a food processor, a hand blender should be sufficient for most recipes. You might also find a potato masher useful, because some recipes call for soups to be lightly mashed or blended to give them a coarse texture.

Ice-cube trays

You can use these to store small amounts of soup, and they are also good for storing stock. This means that you can make a large amount and then use a number of cubes, depending on the amount of soup you're preparing at the time.

finishing touches

Because soup is such a versatile dish, you may be serving it for anything from a quick family meal to an impressive starter for a dinner party. In fact, soup is a great choice when you have guests because most of the preparation, and often the cooking, can be done in advance. To make your dish look even more impressive, there are plenty of lovely ideas for garnishes and toppings. Add these to the bowls just before serving to ensure that they stay fresh and crisp.

 Herbs

Fresh herbs add colour and flavour to soups, and you should try to match the herbs used for the garnish to those used in the main recipe. A couple of long chives carefully placed across the centre of the bowl can look very effective, or you could try a dollop of crème fraîche, topped with some snipped chives. Whole basil leaves work well on tomato-based soups, while chopped fresh coriander adds a cool contrast to spicy flavours.

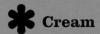 **Cream**

Many soups contain milk or cream, and it's nice to finish these off with a swirl of cream on top. Cream also works well with courgette or tomato soups. A small spoonful of natural yogurt, crème fraîche or soured cream could be used as an alternative. A pinch of paprika can add a colourful contrast to the white crème fraîche and would work well with hearty flavours or spicy soups.

✱ Croûtons

You can buy packets of croûtons if you're really pressed for time, but it's easy to make your own. Simply cut the crusts from a couple of slices of thick, white bread and cut the bread into even-sized squares (you can make these as small or big as you like). Place them on a lightly oiled baking sheet and brush them with a little olive oil. Bake them in a preheated medium-hot oven, 200°C (400°F), Gas Mark 6, for 8–10 minutes or until they are crisp and golden. For a variation, sprinkle over a little grated Parmesan cheese or cut the bread into long, thin strips instead. You can even use biscuit cutters to create different shapes.

Very thin slices of baguette also work well with grated cheese. You can grill these until the cheese has melted and balance one or two on top of each bowl of soup. Alternatively, you can rub bread with garlic as in Onion Soup with Garlic Croûtons (see page 112).

✱ Bread

Instead of the traditional bread roll, you could try toasting pitta breads and cutting them into slices. Arrange these on a plate to serve with the soup. Thin strips of warmed naan bread or flour tortilla are also good for dunking.

✱ Other ideas

Try balancing a couple of rashers of crisp streaky bacon on the soup. Seafood soups look impressive with one or two large prawns in the centre. Very finely chopped onion and tomato make a great finish for chilled summer soups, and a little grated orange rind will add a zing to any soups that include orange juice.

25 g (1 oz) **butter**

3 **shallots**, roughly chopped

1 small **leek**, roughly chopped

1 **celery stick** or piece of **fennel**, roughly chopped

1 kg (2 lb) **white fish** or **shellfish bones, heads and trimmings**

150 ml (¼ pint) **dry white wine**

several sprigs of **parsley**

½ **lemon**, sliced

1 teaspoon **black peppercorns** or **white peppercorns**

1 litre (1¾ pints) **water**

10

PREP

30

COOK

1 litre

1¾ pints

MAKES

Fish stock

Do not use oily fish to make stock because it will make it greasy and give it an overpowering flavour. Fish stock requires less cooking than meat stocks, so take care that you do not overcook it or you will spoil the flavour.

1 Melt the butter in a large, heavy-based saucepan until bubbling.

2 Add all the vegetables and cook over a moderate heat for 5 minutes or until softened but not browned. Add the fish bones, heads and trimmings, wine, parsley, lemon, peppercorns and measured water.

3 Bring to the boil, skimming off the scum that rises to the surface. Reduce the heat and simmer the stock for 20 minutes.

4 Strain, cover and leave to cool. Chill in the refrigerator overnight, then remove and discard the layer of fat that will have set on the surface. Store in the refrigerator for up to 24 hours or freeze immediately.

Chicken stock

10

PREP

120

COOK

Never throw away a chicken carcass. Cooked or raw, it makes a fabulous stock and the basis of so many good soups. Gather up all the bones, skin and pan scrapings from a roast. Alternatively, if you are using a raw carcass, cook it for about 30 minutes in a hot oven first until browned.

1 Pack the chicken carcass into a large, heavy-based saucepan, crushing the bones if necessary to make it fit. Add the trimmings, vegetables, bay leaves and peppercorns. Just cover with cold water.

2 Bring slowly to the boil, skimming off the scum that rises to the surface. Reduce the heat and simmer very gently for 1½–2 hours.

3 Strain, cover and leave to cool. Chill in the refrigerator overnight, then remove and discard the layer of fat that will have set on the surface. Store in the refrigerator for up to 4 days or freeze immediately.

1
litre

1¾
pints

MAKES

1 large **chicken carcass**, including any trimmings, such as the neck, heart and gizzard if available (but not the liver)

1 **onion**, roughly chopped

1 large **carrot**, roughly chopped

several **bay leaves**

1 teaspoon **black peppercorns**

Beef stock

1.75 kg (3½ lb) **beef bones**, chopped into 7 cm (3 inch) pieces

2 **onions**, quartered

2 **carrots**, chopped

2 **celery sticks**, chopped

2 **tomatoes**, chopped

4 litres (7 pints) **water**

10 sprigs of **parsley**

4 sprigs of **thyme**

2 **bay leaves**

8 **black peppercorns**

15

PREP

300

COOK

2 litres

3½ pints

MAKES

When you buy beef, remember to get the bones as well and ask your butcher to cut them into manageable pieces. You can use cheaper cuts of beef and trimmings instead, but that's more expensive than using bones.

1 Put the bones in a large roasting tin and roast in a preheated oven, 230°C (450°F), Gas Mark 8, for 30 minutes or until lightly browned and the fat and juices run, turning occasionally. Add all the vegetables, spoon over the fat from the tin and roast, stirring occasionally, for a further 30 minutes.

2 Transfer the bones and vegetables to a large, heavy-based saucepan. Pour off the fat from the tin and add 150 ml (¼ pint) of the measured water. Set over a low heat and bring to the boil, scraping up any sediment. Pour into the saucepan. Add the remaining water.

3 Bring to the boil, skimming off the scum that rises to the surface. Add the herbs and peppercorns. Partially cover, then reduce the heat and simmer for 4 hours.

4 Strain, cover and leave to cool. Chill in the refrigerator overnight, then remove and discard the layer of fat that will have set on the surface. Store in the refrigerator for up to 4 days or freeze immediately.

Vegetable stock

You can use any combination of vegetables that you like, but make sure that they are fresh. Always include onions, but avoid any with strong flavours, such as cabbage, and starchy ones, such as potatoes, which will make the stock cloudy. In many of the recipes you can use chicken stock instead.

1 Melt the butter in a large, heavy-based saucepan, add all the vegetables and stir well to coat, then cover and cook over a low heat for 10 minutes.

2 Stir in all the herbs and add the measured water. Bring to the boil, then reduce the heat, cover and simmer for 15 minutes.

3 Strain the stock, cover and leave to cool. Chill in the refrigerator overnight. Store the stock in the refrigerator for up to 2 days or freeze immediately.

15

PREP

30

COOK

600 ml

1 pint

MAKES

50 g (2 oz) **butter**

2 **onions**, chopped

2 **leeks**, thinly sliced

2 **carrots**, chopped

2 **celery sticks**, chopped

1 **fennel bulb**, chopped

1 sprig of **thyme**

1 sprig of **marjoram**

1 sprig of **fennel**

4 sprigs of **parsley**

900 ml (1½ pints) **water**

meat and poultry

125 g (4 oz) **butter**

150 g (5 oz) **pancetta** or **streaky bacon**, chopped

2 **onions**, finely chopped

1 **carrot**, chopped

1 **celery stick**, chopped

750 g (1½ lb) can **whole chestnuts**, drained and rinsed

1 tablespoon chopped **rosemary**

2 **bay leaves**

2 **garlic cloves**, halved

salt and **pepper**

sprigs of **rosemary**, to garnish

20

PREP

60

COOK

6

SERVES

herby

Chestnut soup with pancetta and rosemary

We tend to think of chestnuts as a Christmas delicacy, but they are available canned, so you can use them all year round. They add a lovely woody flavour to dishes.

1 Melt the butter in a large, heavy-based saucepan, add the pancetta or bacon and cook over a moderate heat until just starting to brown. Add the onions, carrot and celery and cook for 5–10 minutes or until softened and lightly browned.

2 Add the chestnuts, rosemary, bay leaves and garlic to the pan. Add enough water to cover completely and bring to the boil. Partially cover, reduce the heat and simmer, stirring occasionally, for 30 minutes. The chestnuts should start to disintegrate and thicken the soup. Taste and season well with salt and pepper.

3 Ladle the soup into warm bowls and serve garnished with rosemary sprigs.

Potato and bacon soup

20

PREP

60

COOK

8

SERVES

tasty

The bacon rinds are left on in this recipe because the fat adds lots of flavour to the soup. Always use proper stocks in soups – they are far superior to those made up from stock cubes.

1 Cut the rinds off the bacon and set them aside. Chop the bacon roughly. Heat the oil in a large, heavy-based saucepan, add the rinds and cook over a moderate heat until crisp. Remove with a slotted spoon and discard.

2 Add the chopped bacon, onion and garlic to the bacon fat and cook over a moderate heat, stirring frequently, for 8–10 minutes or until the onion is lightly browned and the bacon fairly crisp.

3 Add the stock, measured water, potatoes, leeks, marjoram, nutmeg, Worcestershire sauce and pepper to taste. Bring to the boil, then reduce the heat, cover and simmer, stirring occasionally, for 25 minutes.

4 In a blender or food processor, blend 600 ml (1 pint) of the soup for 2 seconds. Return to the pan. Stir well and simmer gently for a further 10 minutes. Season to taste with salt and pepper. Stir in the parsley (if using) and serve immediately in warm soup bowls.

175 g (6 oz) rashers of **smoked bacon**, rinds on

1 tablespoon **olive oil**

1 **onion**, finely chopped

2 **garlic cloves**, finely chopped

600 ml (1 pint) **Chicken Stock** (see page 17)

1.2 litres (2 pints) **water**

750 g (1½ lb) **potatoes**, diced

3 **leeks**, sliced

1 teaspoon chopped **marjoram**

¼ teaspoon **grated nutmeg**

1 teaspoon **Worcestershire sauce**

3–4 tablespoons finely chopped **parsley** (optional)

salt and **pepper**

1 teaspoon **olive oil**

2 rashers of **smoked bacon**, chopped

2 **garlic cloves**, crushed

1 **onion**, chopped

few sprigs of **thyme** or **lemon thyme**

2 x 400 g (13 oz) cans **cannellini beans**, rinsed and drained

600 ml (1 pint) **Vegetable Stock** (see page 19)

2 tablespoons chopped **parsley**

pepper

crusty **bread**, to serve

5

PREP

15

COOK

4

SERVES

quick

Smoky bacon and white bean soup

Beans and other pulses make a wonderful addition to soups. Not only do they add bulk, but they also absorb the flavours from other ingredients. Canned beans are great to use for convenience, but you could soak dried beans and use those, if you prefer.

1 Heat the oil in a large, heavy-based saucepan, add the bacon, garlic and onion and cook over a moderate heat for about 3–4 minutes or until the bacon is beginning to brown and the onion to soften.

2 Add the thyme or lemon thyme and cook for a further 1 minute. Add the beans and stock and bring to the boil, then reduce the heat and simmer for 10 minutes.

3 In a blender or food processor, blend the soup with the parsley and pepper to taste until smooth. Return to the pan and reheat gently. Serve the soup in warm bowls with crusty bread.

Bacon and turnip soup

The humble turnip has suffered from neglect in kitchens in recent years, but this hearty vegetable is perfect for soups, stews and casseroles. Here, it complements the rich, salty taste of the smoked bacon.

15

PREP

45

COOK

6

SERVES

thick

25 g (1 oz) **butter**

125 g (4 oz) rindless **smoked bacon**, roughly chopped

1 **onion**, roughly chopped

375 g (12 oz) **potatoes**, chopped

750 g (1½ lb) **turnips**, chopped

1.2 litres (2 pints) **Chicken Stock** (see page 17)

1 **bay leaf**

1 small sprig of **thyme**

150 ml (¼ pint) **milk**

salt and **pepper**

finely chopped **parsley**, to garnish

1 Melt the butter in a large, heavy-based saucepan, add the bacon and cook over a moderate heat until crisp and golden. Remove with a slotted spoon and reserve.

2 Add the onion, potatoes and turnips to the bacon fat and cook over a low heat for about 5 minutes. Add the stock, bay leaf and thyme and bring to the boil, then reduce the heat and cook for 30–35 minutes or until all the vegetables are tender. Remove and discard the bay leaf and thyme.

3 In a blender or food processor, blend the soup in batches until smooth, then transfer it to a clean saucepan. Add the reserved bacon and the milk and reheat gently without boiling. Serve the soup in warm soup bowls, sprinkled with a little finely chopped parsley.

2 tablespoons **olive oil**

3 rashers of rindless **smoked bacon**, chopped

2 **onions**, finely chopped

600 ml (1 pint) **Chicken Stock** (see page 17)

900 ml (1½ pints) **water**

625 g (1¼ lb) **potatoes**, cut into 1 cm (½ inch) cubes

4 tablespoons **plain flour**

50 g (2 oz) **Gruyère cheese**, grated

1 tablespoon **medium dry sherry**

1 teaspoon **Worcestershire sauce**

3 tablespoons finely chopped **parsley**

salt and **pepper**

20

PREP

30

COOK

6

SERVES

tasty

Gruyère soup with bacon and potatoes

Parsley makes the perfect garnish for this rich, flavourful soup, giving it a touch of vibrant colour and a contrasting crispness.

1 Heat the oil in a large, heavy-based saucepan, add the bacon and onions and cook over a moderate heat until the onion is pale golden. Add the stock, 600 ml (1 pint) of the measured water and the potatoes and bring to the boil, then reduce the heat, cover and simmer for about 15 minutes or until the potatoes are tender.

2 In a small bowl, whisk the flour with the remaining water and stir the mixture into the soup. Cover and simmer, stirring frequently, for a further 5 minutes.

3 In a blender or food processor, blend the Gruyère with 300 ml (½ pint) of the soup. Return to the pan and add the sherry, Worcestershire sauce and pepper to taste. Simmer for 3–5 minutes. Stir in the parsley and serve immediately in warm soup bowls.

Green lentil and bacon soup

Also known as Continental lentils, green lentils are, as the name suggests, popular in European cooking, and they make a wholesome soup that is a good source of protein. Unlike orange and brown Indian lentils, which quickly cook down to a purée, green lentils retain their shape after cooking.

20

PREP

75

COOK

6

SERVES

hearty

25 g (1 oz) **butter**

125 g (4 oz) rindless **smoked bacon**, finely chopped

1 **garlic clove**, finely chopped

1 **onion**, finely chopped

425 g (14 oz) **green lentils**, washed and drained

1 **celery stick**, sliced

1 large **carrot**, diced

1 sprig of **parsley**

1 sprig of **thyme**

1 **bay leaf**

1.2 litres (2 pints) **Chicken Stock** (see page 17)

900 ml (1½ pints) **water**

1 slice of **lemon**

salt and **pepper**

1 Melt the butter in a large, heavy-based saucepan, add the bacon, garlic and onion and cook over a moderate to high heat for 5 minutes.

2 Reduce the heat and add the lentils, celery, carrot, parsley, thyme and bay leaf to the pan. Pour in the stock and measured water and bring to the boil, skimming off the scum that rises to the surface. Add the lemon slice.

3 Reduce the heat, cover and simmer, stirring occasionally, for 55–60 minutes. Add a little more water if the soup is too thick. Remove and discard the parsley, thyme, bay leaf and lemon slice.

4 In a blender or food processor, blend 600 ml (1 pint) of the soup until smooth. Return to the pan, stir well and season to taste with salt and pepper. Reheat gently. Transfer to warm soup bowls and serve immediately.

375 g (12 oz) **split yellow peas**, soaked overnight in cold water

2 tablespoons **olive oil**

3 **chorizo sausages**, thinly sliced

1 **onion**, chopped

2 **garlic cloves**, finely chopped

1.2 litres (2 pints) **Chicken Stock** (see page 17)

900 ml (1½ pints) **water**

1 **bay leaf**

1 sprig of **thyme**

3 **carrots**, quartered lengthways and thinly sliced

salt

20*

PREP

120

COOK

6

SERVES

spicy

Yellow pea soup with chorizo

Chorizo is a spicy sausage, originating from Spain and Latin America, made with pork and seasoned with garlic, paprika and hot peppers. It gives this traditional pulse-based soup a special bite.

1 Drain the soaked split peas, rinse under cold running water and drain again.

2 Heat the oil in a large, heavy-based saucepan, add the chorizo and cook over a moderate heat for 5 minutes or until browned. Remove with a slotted spoon and leave to drain on kitchen paper. Pour off all but 1 tablespoon of the fat in the pan.

3 Add the onion and garlic to the pan and cook over a moderate heat for 5 minutes or until softened. Add the split peas, stock, measured water, bay leaf and thyme and bring to the boil, skimming off the scum that rises to the surface. Reduce the heat, partially cover and simmer, stirring occasionally, for 1¼ hours.

4 Add the carrots and cook for a further 30 minutes or until tender. Season to taste with salt. Remove and discard the bay leaf, add the reserved chorizo and cook for a further 10 minutes. Serve immediately in warm, deep soup bowls.

* Plus overnight soaking

Beef and noodle broth

15

PREP

10

COOK

2

SERVES

stylish

This nourishing soup relies on good, well-flavoured stock and is ideal for using up any beef or chicken stock that you might have in the freezer. When you are slicing the beef, cut it across the grain so that it falls into tender, succulent slices.

1 Trim any fat from the beef. Mix the ginger with 1 teaspoon of the soy sauce and smooth over both sides of the beef.

2 Cook the rice noodles according to the packet instructions. Drain and rinse under cold running water.

3 Pour the stock into a saucepan, add the chilli, garlic and sugar and bring to a gentle simmer, then cover and cook over a low heat for 5 minutes.

4 Heat the oil in a small, heavy-based frying pan, add the beef and cook for 2 minutes on each side. Transfer to a board. When cool enough to handle, cut in half lengthways, then cut across into thin strips.

5 Add the noodles, sugar snap peas, basil and remaining soy sauce to the soup and heat gently for 1 minute. Stir in the beef and serve immediately in warm soup bowls.

300 g (10 oz) **rump** or **sirloin steak**

15 g (½ oz) fresh **root ginger**, peeled and grated

2 teaspoons **light soy sauce**

50 g (2 oz) dried **vermicelli rice noodles**

600 ml (1 pint) **Beef Stock** (see page 18)

1 **red chilli**, deseeded and finely chopped

1 **garlic clove**, thinly sliced

2 teaspoons **caster sugar**

2 teaspoons **vegetable oil**

75 g (3 oz) **sugar snap peas**, halved lengthways

small handful of **Thai basil**, torn into pieces

50 g (2 oz) **chickpeas**, soaked overnight in cold water

50 g (2 oz) **black-eyed beans**, soaked overnight in cold water

50 g (2 oz) **bulgar wheat**

500 g (1 lb) **neck of lamb**, cut into 4 pieces

4 tablespoons **olive oil**

1 **onion**, chopped

2 **carrots**, chopped

400 g (13 oz) can chopped **tomatoes**

4 small **red chillies**

4 sprigs of **thyme**

1 teaspoon each **ground coriander**, **ground cumin** and **ground cinnamon**

½ teaspoon each **dried mint** and **dried oregano**

salt and **pepper**

TO SERVE:

olive oil

crusty **bread**

15*

PREP

150

COOK

6

SERVES

easy

Spiced chickpea and lamb soup

The great thing about this richly spiced soup is the ease with which it is prepared and cooked. All the ingredients are put straight into a casserole (traditionally an earthenware dish) and baked until tender.

1 Drain the soaked chickpeas and beans, rinse under cold running water and drain again. Put the chickpeas and beans in separate saucepans, cover with plenty of cold water and bring to the boil. Reduce the heat and simmer for 1 hour, then drain and reserve the liquid.

2 Put the cooked chickpeas and beans in a clay pot or casserole, add all the remaining ingredients and cover with the reserved liquid. Add extra water to cover if necessary.

3 Cover the pot or casserole with a tight-fitting lid and cook in a preheated oven, 180°F (350°F), Gas Mark 4, for 1½ hours or until the meat and vegetables are tender.

4 Spoon the soup into warm bowls, drizzle with olive oil and serve accompanied with some crusty bread.

* Plus overnight soaking

Consommé

15
PREP

120
COOK

6
SERVES

classic

375 g (12 oz) lean **shin of beef**

1.2 litres (2 pints) **Beef Stock** (see page 18)

1 **onion**, roughly chopped

1 **celery stick**, chopped

2 sprigs of **parsley**

6 **black peppercorns**

1 tablespoon **medium dry sherry** (optional)

1 **egg white**, lightly beaten

1 **eggshell**, lightly crushed

1 teaspoon **caster sugar**

salt (optional)

This classic soup can be served hot or chilled. If chilled, it will turn to jelly, in which case it should be broken up with a fork before being served sprinkled with finely chopped fresh herbs, such as parsley, chervil or chives. Consommé makes an ideal starter if followed by a substantial second course.

1 Cut the beef into small pieces and put in a large, heavy-based saucepan. Add the stock, onion, celery, parsley and peppercorns. Bring to the boil, then reduce the heat, partially cover and simmer for 1½ hours. Carefully strain the liquid through a muslin cloth or very fine wire sieve into a separate saucepan. Add the sherry (if using).

2 To clear the consommé, add the egg white and crushed eggshell. Simmer for a further 30 minutes, then strain again.

3 Transfer the consommé to a clean sauce-pan and add the sugar and salt (if using). Heat, stirring, until the sugar has dissolved. Serve the consommé hot or well chilled in bouillon cups.

1 kg (2 lb) lean **stewing beef**, cut into cubes

250 g (8 oz) lean **pork**, cut into cubes

2.5 litres (4 pints) **water**

24 **okra**, trimmed and chopped

500 g (1 lb) **kale**, stalks discarded, roughly chopped

2 **green peppers**, cored, deseeded and chopped

2 **spring onions**, roughly chopped

1 sprig of **thyme**

¼ teaspoon **cayenne pepper**

500 g (1 lb) **yellow yams**, peeled and sliced

1 large **potato**, sliced

1 **garlic clove**, finely chopped

salt

20

PREP

70

COOK

6

SERVES

exotic

Jamaican pepperpot soup

This filling, wholesome soup comes from the sunny Caribbean, but it is a perfect dish for a gloomy winter's day. Okra, sometimes known as ladies' fingers, and yams give the soup a distinctive, rather exotic flavour.

1 Combine the meat with the measured water in a large saucepan. Bring to the boil, then reduce the heat, partially cover and simmer for about 30 minutes.

2 Add the okra, kale, green peppers and spring onions to the soup with the thyme and cayenne pepper. Partially cover and cook over a moderate heat for 15 minutes.

3 Add the yams, potato and garlic and cook for a further 20 minutes or until the yams and potato are tender. Add more water if the soup is too thick. Season to taste with salt and serve in warm bowls.

Beef and cabbage soup with mustard

The spices and fresh herbs in this soup add a twist to a traditional combination. If you are using dried herbs, the general rule is that you should add half the quantity of fresh herbs given here.

1 Heat the oil in a large, heavy-based saucepan, add the beef and cook over a moderate to high heat for 2 minutes, turning each piece once. Add the onions and cook, stirring frequently, for 3 minutes.

2 Add the stock, caraway seeds, marjoram and thyme to the soup and bring to the boil, then reduce the heat, partially cover and simmer for 35–40 minutes. Add the potatoes and cabbage, partially cover and cook for a further 25 minutes.

3 Using a slotted spoon, transfer the beef to a board. When cool enough to handle, cut into 1 cm (½ inch) dice. Return to the soup. Stir in the mustard and cook for 2 minutes without boiling. Serve immediately in warm bowls.

15

PREP

75

COOK

6

SERVES

filling

2 tablespoons **olive oil**

250 g (8 oz) lean **beef**, in 1–2 pieces

2 **onions**, finely chopped

1.5 litres (2½ pints) **Beef Stock** (see page 18)

2 teaspoons **caraway seeds**

1 teaspoon chopped **marjoram**

½ teaspoon chopped **thyme**

175 g (6 oz) **potatoes**, diced

175–200 g (6–7 oz) **Savoy cabbage**, finely shredded

1 tablespoon **Dijon mustard**

50 g (2 oz) **butter**

1 large **onion**, chopped

475–500 g (15–16 oz) can **sauerkraut**, drained and chopped

2 tablespoons **paprika**

1 tablespoon **caraway seeds**

1.5 litres (2½ pints) **Vegetable Stock** (see page 19)

2 tablespoons **tomato purée**

¼ teaspoon **caster sugar**

375 g (12 oz) **potatoes**, diced

salt

TO GARNISH:

4–6 tablespoons **soured cream**

1–2 tablespoons snipped **chives**

10

PREP

50

COOK

6

SERVES

spicy

Hungarian sauerkraut soup

The unique blend of sweet paprika, tangy sauerkraut and fragrant caraway seeds gives this soup a distinctive flavour. Use sweet Hungarian paprika if you can find it.

1 Melt the butter in a large, heavy-based saucepan, add the onion and cook over a moderate heat for 5 minutes or until softened but not browned.

2 Add the sauerkraut, paprika and caraway seeds and cook, stirring constantly, for 2 minutes. Add the stock, tomato purée, sugar and potatoes. Stir, bring to the boil and season to taste with salt. Reduce the heat, cover and simmer for about 45 minutes.

3 In a small bowl, mix the soured cream with the chives. Spoon the soup into warm bowls, garnish each portion with 1 tablespoon of the soured cream mixture and serve immediately.

White cabbage soup with meatballs

Cabbage, in all its varieties, is a favourite ingredient in European peasant soups. In this delicious, hearty dish, the smooth, hard-packed white cabbage, also known as Dutch cabbage, is the chief component.

25
PREP

50
COOK

4
SERVES

hearty

1 Discard the outer leaves and core of the cabbage. Shred the cabbage leaves roughly.

2 Melt the butter in a large, heavy-based saucepan, add the cabbage and sugar and cook, stirring constantly, until the cabbage is golden. Add the stock, allspice berries and peppercorns, cover and simmer for 30–35 minutes or until the cabbage is tender. Add salt to taste.

3 Make the meatballs. Put the breadcrumbs in a bowl, add the measured water and leave to soak for 3 minutes. Add all the remaining ingredients and stir the mixture vigorously with a fork until smooth. Shape the mixture into balls the size of walnuts.

4 Bring the soup to the boil. Drop in the meatballs one by one. Reduce the heat and simmer for 10 minutes. Transfer to a warm tureen and serve in large, warm soup bowls.

1 **white cabbage**, about 875 g (1¾ lb)

50 g (2 oz) **butter**

2 teaspoons **caster sugar**

1.5 litres (2½ pints) **Beef Stock** (see page 18)

3 **allspice berries**

6 **white peppercorns**

salt

MEATBALLS:

2 tablespoons **dried white breadcrumbs**

150 ml (¼ pint) **water**

250 g (8 oz) **lean minced veal**

250 g (8 oz) **lean minced pork**

2 **egg yolks**

1 teaspoon **salt**

¼ teaspoon **white pepper**

1 teaspoon **Worcestershire sauce**

1 teaspoon **Dijon mustard**

Oxtail soup

20

PREP

255

COOK

6

SERVES

classic

50 g (2 oz) **butter**, **lard** or **dripping**

1 **oxtail**, about 1 kg (2 lb), cut into 5 cm (2 inch) pieces, excess fat removed

375 g (12 oz) **onions**, chopped

3 **celery sticks**, chopped

250 g (8 oz) **carrots**, chopped

1 **bay leaf**, crushed

6 **black peppercorns**, crushed

2 **cloves**

¼ teaspoon **caster sugar**

3 litres (5½ pints) **water**

1 tablespoon **plain flour**

milk, for mixing

150 ml (¼ pint) **red wine** or 2 tablespoons **dry sherry**

salt and **pepper**

finely chopped **parsley**, to garnish

This classic soup has stood the test of time, remaining a firm favourite today. Containing peppercorns, bay and cloves, it's packed full of wonderful flavours, the lengthy cooking time allowing these to develop to the full.

1 Melt the butter, lard or dripping in a large, heavy-based saucepan, add the oxtail and onions and cook over a moderate heat, turning the oxtail once, until lightly browned.

2 Add the celery, carrots, bay leaf, peppercorns, cloves and sugar. Season to taste with salt and pepper. Pour in the measured water and bring to the boil. Reduce the heat, cover and simmer for about 4 hours or until the oxtail is tender.

3 Take the oxtail pieces from the pan, strip the meat from the bones, shred and return the meat to the pan. Discard the bones.

4 In a small bowl, mix the flour with enough milk to make a thin paste. Whisk it into the soup, stirring until the soup thickens. Add the wine or sherry and bring the soup slowly to the boil. Serve the soup immediately in warm soup bowls, garnished with finely chopped parsley.

Mulligatawny soup

The word mulligatawny is a corruption of the Tamil word **milagu-tuanni**, which roughly means 'pepper water'. It was introduced to the British Raj by Indian cooks during the 19th century and became known by its present name. The soup should be highly flavoured and very spicy.

1 In a blender or food processor, blend the onion, garlic and ginger with the dry spices to a smooth paste.

2 Heat the oil in a large, heavy-based saucepan, add the onion paste and cook over a moderate heat, stirring, for 2–3 minutes. Add the chicken breasts and cook, stirring, for 1–2 minutes.

3 Slowly add the stock and water, stirring constantly. Add the rice and lentils. Simmer for 15–20 minutes or until the rice is tender.

4 Remove the chicken, cut it into small pieces and set aside. In a blender or food processor, blend 900 ml (1½ pints) of the soup until smooth. Return to the pan and stir well. Add a little more water if the soup is too thick.

5 Add the lemon juice, creamed coconut and reserved chicken. Stir well and reheat gently, without boiling, for 3–5 minutes. Ladle into warm soup bowls, garnish each portion with a lemon slice and serve immediately.

20 PREP

35 COOK

6 SERVES

spicy

1 **onion**, chopped

2 **garlic cloves**, chopped

2.5 cm (1 inch) piece of fresh **root ginger**, peeled and chopped

1 teaspoon **ground coriander**

¼ teaspoon **cayenne pepper** (or to taste)

½ teaspoon **ground cumin**

1 teaspoon **ground turmeric**

4 teaspoons **vegetable oil**

3 boneless, skinless **chicken breasts**, halved

1.2 litres (2 pints) **Chicken Stock** (see page 17)

1.2 litres (2 pints) **water**

50 g (2 oz) **white long-grain rice**

125 g (4 oz) **red lentils**, washed and drained

1 tablespoon **lemon juice**

2 tablespoons grated **creamed coconut**

salt

6 **lemon slices**, to garnish

4 tablespoons **olive oil**

1 **garlic clove**, chopped

1 **onion**, chopped

1.2 litres (2 pints) **Beef Stock** (see page 18)

750 ml (1¼ pints) **water**

300 g (10 oz) lean **pork**, cut into 1.5 cm (¾ inch) strips

2 **carrots**, chopped

300 g (10 oz) **Savoy cabbage**, roughly chopped

125 g (4 oz) **pearl barley**

300 g (10 oz) **potatoes**, cut into 1 cm (½ inch) cubes

salt and **pepper**

PREP 15

COOK 55

SERVES 6

filling

Barley soup with pork and cabbage

The pearl barley is a lovely complement to the rich pork, and the cabbage adds colour to this delicious winter soup. Use any spring cabbage if you cannot find a Savoy.

1 Heat the oil in a large, heavy-based saucepan, add the garlic and onion and cook over a moderate heat for about 5 minutes or until softened.

2 Add the stock, measured water, pork, carrots, cabbage and barley and bring to the boil. Reduce the heat, cover and simmer for 20 minutes.

3 Add the potatoes and season to taste with salt and pepper. Add a little more water if the soup is too thick. Cover and simmer, stirring occasionally, for a further 30 minutes. Serve immediately in warm soup bowls.

Goulash soup

Goulash stew and soup originated in Hungary and later became popular dishes in Austria. Although several variations exist, the chief ingredients remain the paprika and caraway seeds that lend the soup its uniquely aromatic flavour.

1 Heat the oil in a large, heavy-based saucepan, add the beef, in batches, and cook over a moderate heat until browned. As each batch browns, remove with a slotted spoon and drain on kitchen paper. Add the onions, garlic and celery to the pan and cook for 5 minutes or until softened.

2 Remove from the heat and stir in the paprika, caraway seeds, stock and measured water. Add the thyme, bay leaves, Tabasco sauce and tomato purée. Stir well and add the browned beef. Bring to the boil, then reduce the heat, partially cover and simmer for about 30 minutes.

3 Add the potatoes and carrots and simmer for a further 30 minutes or until the potatoes are tender. Remove and discard the bay leaves. Spoon the soup into warm soup bowls, garnish each portion with soured cream, if liked, and serve immediately.

15
PREP

75
COOK

6
SERVES

spicy

3 tablespoons **vegetable oil**

750 g (1½ lb) boneless lean **beef**, cut into 2.5 cm (1 inch) strips

2 **onions**, chopped

2 **garlic cloves**, crushed

2 **celery sticks**, sliced

3 tablespoons **paprika**

1 tablespoon **caraway seeds**

1.2 litres (2 pints) **Beef Stock** (see page 18)

600 ml (1 pint) **water**

¼ teaspoon **dried thyme**

2 **bay leaves**

¼ teaspoon **Tabasco sauce** (or to taste)

3 tablespoons **tomato purée**

250 g (8 oz) **potatoes**, cut into 1 cm (½ inch) cubes

3 **carrots**, cut into 1 cm (½ inch) cubes

6–8 teaspoons **soured cream** (optional)

250 g (8 oz) **pork** fillet

1.8 litres (3 pints)
Chicken Stock
(see page 17)

3 tablespoons **soy sauce**

2 tablespoons **dry sherry**

2 tablespoons **sesame oil**

5 cm (2 inch) piece of
fresh **root ginger**, peeled
and cut into matchsticks

2 **garlic cloves**, crushed

1¼ teaspoons **ground
coriander**

1 teaspoon **ground
turmeric**

¼ teaspoon **chilli powder**

125 g (4 oz) **egg noodles**

125 g (4 oz) **creamed
coconut**, dissolved in 300
ml (½ pint) boiling water

1 **green pepper**, cored,
deseeded and cut into
matchsticks

5 **spring onions**, sliced

250 g (8 oz) **green
beans**, halved

2 **carrots**, cut into thin
matchsticks

125 g (4 oz) **bean sprouts**

salt and **pepper**

PREP

COOK

SERVES

Laksa

This soup, originally from Singapore, is a substantial mixture of pork, egg noodles, vegetables, coconut and spices and could be served as a main course.

1 Put the pork, 1.5 litres (2½ pints) of the stock, the soy sauce and sherry in a large saucepan and bring to the boil, skimming off the scum that rises to the surface. Reduce the heat, partially cover and simmer for about 20 minutes or until the pork is just tender.

2 Meanwhile, heat the oil in a separate large saucepan, add the ginger, garlic and dry spices and cook over a moderate heat, stirring, for 5 minutes. Remove from the heat.

3 Remove the pork from the liquid. Add the noodles and return to the boil. Cover tightly, remove from the heat and leave to stand for 5 minutes. Cut the pork into thin, short strips.

4 Drain the noodles, adding the liquid to the spice mixture. Add the remaining stock and creamed coconut and bring to the boil. Add the vegetables and simmer for 8–10 minutes.

5 Cut the noodles into short pieces. Add to the soup with the pork and bean sprouts. Season to taste, bring to the boil and cook for 1–2 minutes. Serve in warm soup bowls.

Spicy chilli bean soup

15*

PREP

This hearty soup is packed full of highly flavoured ingredients, including delicious sausages, which add a rich, rounded flavour. Serve with warmed flour tortillas, sliced into thick strips.

COOK

1 Heat the oil in a large, heavy-based saucepan, add the sausage slices and cook over a moderate heat for 5 minutes or until browned. Remove with a slotted spoon and leave to drain on kitchen paper.

2 Add the onion to the pan and cook for 5 minutes or until softened. Add the chilli powder, cumin and thyme and cook, stirring constantly, for 1 minute. Add the beans, bay leaf and stock. Bring to the boil, then reduce the heat, cover and simmer for 1 hour.

3 Add the garlic, red pepper and tomatoes, cover and simmer, stirring occasionally, for a further 1 hour. Add the sausage slices, then season to taste with salt and cook, stirring frequently, for a further 5 minutes. Serve in warm soup bowls.

4

SERVES

hearty

2 tablespoons **olive oil**

4 small or 2 large **Kabanos sausages**, thinly sliced

1 **onion**, chopped

1 tablespoon mild **chilli powder** (or to taste)

1 teaspoon **ground cumin**

¼ teaspoon **dried thyme**

250 g (8 oz) **pinto beans**, soaked overnight in cold water, rinsed and drained

1 **bay leaf**

1.2 litres (2 pints) **Chicken Stock** (see page 17)

2 **garlic cloves**, crushed

1 large **red pepper**, cored, deseeded and chopped

400 g (13 oz) can chopped **tomatoes**

salt

* Plus overnight soaking

Pot-au-feu

1 kg (2 lb) **clod** or **shin of beef** with bones, excess fat removed

1 teaspoon **salt**

1 **bouquet garni**

6 **black peppercorns**, crushed

1 unpeeled **onion**, studded with 4 **cloves**

1 **garlic clove**, crushed

3 **carrots**, chopped

2 **celery sticks**, sliced

3 **leeks**, sliced

500 g (1 lb) **potatoes**, diced

3 tablespoons finely chopped **parsley**, to garnish

15

PREP

220

COOK

4

SERVES

classic

Pot-au-feu is often referred to as the national soup of France. Although the French treat it as a main course and usually serve the meat separately, there are no firm rules when it comes to preparing this substantial dish, and in this recipe it is more of a soup than a main course. Clod is meat cut from the neck.

1 Put the beef and bones in a large saucepan and add cold water to cover. Add the salt and bring to the boil, skimming off the scum that rises to the surface.

2 Reduce the heat and add the bouquet garni, peppercorns, studded onion and the garlic. Partially cover and simmer for about 2½ hours or until the meat is almost tender. Skim from time to time if necessary. Check occasionally if the water level in the saucepan falls and add more water.

3 Remove and discard the bones, bouquet garni and studded onion. Add the vegetables and simmer for a further 1 hour or until all the vegetables are tender. Remove the beef, cut it into pieces, then return to the soup and simmer until heated through. Serve the soup in large, warm soup plates, garnished with the parsley.

Game broth

Game includes partridge, wood pigeon and pheasant. Because the season is relatively short, it's not always easy to get fresh game, but you can use frozen meat instead. Remember to allow plenty of time for defrosting before you need it.

1 Melt the butter in a large, heavy-based saucepan, add the game trimmings or leftovers, setting the breast of game aside, with the beef, ham, onion, celery and carrot. Cook over a moderate heat, stirring frequently, for about 8 minutes or until the vegetables begin to brown.

2 Add the stock, bouquet garni, bay leaf, juniper berries, peppercorns and parsley to the pan. Bring to the boil, then reduce the heat, partially cover and simmer for about 2 hours. Add more water if the liquid reduces too much.

3 Strain the liquid through a fine sieve into a clean saucepan. Discard the solids in the sieve. Stir the sherry into the broth and season to taste with salt. Add the reserved breast of game and simmer until heated through. Serve the broth in warm soup bowls.

15
PREP

135
COOK

6
SERVES

posh

50 g (2 oz) **butter**

500 g (1 lb) cooked **game**, trimmings or leftovers, plus 250 g (8 oz) cooked **breast of game**, cut into thin strips

250 g (8 oz) lean **beef**, thinly cut across the grain

50 g (2 oz) lean cooked **ham**, finely chopped

1 **onion**, chopped

1 **celery stick**, sliced

1 **carrot**, chopped

2 litres (3½ pints) **Beef Stock** (see page 18)

1 **bouquet garni**

1 **bay leaf**

3 **juniper berries**

6 **black peppercorns**

2 sprigs of **parsley**

2 tablespoons **dry sherry**

salt

Avgolemono

10

PREP

50

COOK

2 **chicken quarters**, each about 375 g (12 oz)

2 **carrots**, chopped

1 small **onion**, sliced

1 **celery stick**

2 **bay leaves**

6 **white peppercorns**

1.2 litres (2 pints) **water**

50 g (2 oz) **white long-grain rice**

2 **egg yolks**

3 tablespoons **lemon juice**

4 tablespoons chopped **parsley**

salt and **pepper**

4

SERVES

light

This lemon, chicken and egg soup is made throughout Greece. The eggs thicken the soup as it is heated, but you must be careful not to boil the soup because otherwise the eggs will curdle.

1 Put the chicken, carrots, onion, celery, bay leaves, peppercorns and measured water into a large, heavy-based saucepan. Bring slowly to the boil, skimming the scum that rises to the surface, then reduce the heat and simmer gently for 30 minutes.

2 Strain the stock into a clean saucepan. Cut the chicken into bite-sized pieces and set aside. Add the rice to the stock and simmer for 15 minutes or until tender.

3 In a small bowl, beat together the egg yolks, lemon juice and 2 tablespoons of the stock, then gradually whisk the mixture into the stock in the pan. Add the reserved chicken and parsley. Season to taste with salt and pepper. Reheat gently without boiling and serve hot in warm soup bowls.

Chicken and sweetcorn soup

This soup originally came from southern China, but it is extremely popular in the West. The creamed-style sweetcorn and canned sweetcorn kernels give it texture, and it is thickened with a minimum of cornflour.

1 Put the 1.5 litres (2½ pints) stock in a large, heavy-based saucepan and bring to the boil. Add the creamed-style sweetcorn and sweetcorn kernels, then reduce the heat and simmer for 5 minutes.

2 Add the chicken to the pan, then return the soup to the boil. Add the pepper. Blend the cornflour with the 2 tablespoons stock, slowly stir into the soup and simmer until slightly thickened. Remove from the heat.

3 Slowly drizzle in the beaten eggs, stirring constantly, ideally with chopsticks (stirring helps to form the egg into fine threads). Serve immediately in warm soup bowls.

10
PREP

20
COOK

4
SERVES

quick

1.5 litres (2½ pints) **Chicken Stock** (see page 17), plus 2 tablespoons

275 g (9 oz) can creamed-style **sweetcorn**

275 g (9 oz) can **sweetcorn kernels**, drained

100 g (3½ oz) cooked **chicken**, finely shredded

½ teaspoon **white pepper**

2 teaspoons **cornflour**

2 **eggs**, beaten

2 tablespoons extra virgin **olive oil**

1 **onion**, finely chopped

1 **garlic clove**, finely chopped

150 ml (¼ pint) **dry white wine**

600 ml (1 pint) **Chicken Stock** (see page 17)

4 boneless, skinless **chicken breasts**, each about 200 g (7 oz)

200 g (7 oz) **broad beans**, thawed if frozen

200 g (7 oz) **peas**, thawed if frozen

4 tablespoons chopped **chives**, **mint**, **oregano** or **parsley**

salt and **pepper**

15

PREP

16

COOK

4

SERVES

simple

Chicken with vegetable broth

This recipe really needs a good-quality stock. If you do not have time to make your own, look out for fresh stocks in the chiller section of large supermarkets and at good butchers.

1 Heat the oil in a large, nonstick frying pan, add the onion and garlic and cook over a moderate heat for 5 minutes. Add the wine and boil to reduce by half. Add the stock and chicken and bring to a gentle simmer. Cover and cook for 8 minutes. Remove the chicken from the pan, wrap it in foil and keep warm.

2 Add the beans and peas to the stock and cook for 2–3 minutes or until tender. Add the herbs and salt and pepper to taste.

3 Spoon the vegetables and broth into 4 large, warm soup bowls. Slice the chicken and arrange in the bowls. Serve immediately.

Turkey and vegetable soup

25

PREP

120

COOK

8

SERVES

feast

This soup proves that turkey shouldn't be eaten just on Christmas day! The drumstick contains both white and dark meat, so it will add depth of flavour to the finished dish.

1 Put the drumstick in a large, heavy-based saucepan. Add the measured water, studded onion, parsley sprigs, bouquet garni, salt, thyme and marjoram and bring to the boil. Reduce the heat, partially cover and simmer for 45 minutes.

2 Add the chopped onion, carrots and celery and simmer over a low to moderate heat for 30 minutes, then add the lentils, potatoes, leeks and turnips. Simmer until all the vegetables are tender. Remove the drumstick and leave to cool. Remove and discard the bouquet garni, studded onion and parsley, thyme and marjoram stalks.

3 Cut the turkey meat off the bone, and remove and discard the skin. Carefully remove and discard any small bones. Cut the meat into small pieces and return to the pan. Add the soy sauce and season to taste with pepper. Reheat thoroughly and serve in a warm soup tureen, garnished with parsley.

1 large **turkey drumstick**, about 750 g (1½ lb)

2.5 litres (4 pints) **water**

1 small unpeeled **onion**, studded with 4 **cloves**, plus 1 large **onion**, peeled and chopped

2 sprigs of **parsley**

1 **bouquet garni**

1 teaspoon **salt**

1 sprig of **thyme**

1 sprig of **marjoram**

3 **carrots**, chopped

2 **celery sticks**, sliced

250 g (8 oz) **red lentils**, washed and drained

250 g (8 oz) **potatoes**, cut into 1 cm (½ inch) cubes

3 **leeks**, sliced

3 **turnips**, cut into 1 cm (½ inch) cubes

2 tablespoons **light soy sauce**

pepper

3–4 tablespoons finely chopped **parsley**, to garnish

fish and shellfish

Mussel soup

2 tablespoons **olive oil**

2 **onions**, chopped

2 **garlic cloves**, crushed

1 **red chilli**, chopped

150 g (5 oz) piece of **green bacon**, chopped

1 kg (2 lb) **mussels**, scrubbed and debearded

2 x 400 g (13 oz) cans chopped **tomatoes**

375 ml (13 fl oz) **dry white wine**

good pinch of **saffron threads**

handful of **flat leaf parsley**, roughly chopped

salt and **pepper**

20

PREP

10

COOK

4

SERVES

tasty

It is very important to clean the live mussels thoroughly before using to get rid of any debris. The beards can be pulled off with a sharp tug. Bacon, garlic, chilli and wine are ideal flavourings for the shellfish.

1 Heat the oil in a large, heavy-based saucepan, add the onions, garlic, chilli and bacon and cook over a moderate heat for 5 minutes.

2 Discard any mussels that are broken or open, or that do not close when tapped on a work surface.

3 Add the mussels, tomatoes, wine and saffron to the pan, mix well and season to taste with salt and pepper. Cover tightly and simmer for 5 minutes or until all the mussel shells have opened. Discard any mussels that have not opened. Add the parsley and stir well. Serve the soup immediately in warm soup bowls.

Mussel chowder

Use the small, plump European mussels for this smooth, creamy soup – the large New Zealand mussels are not suitable.

1 Heat the oil in a large, heavy-based saucepan, add the bacon and cook over a moderate heat until browned. Add the onions, celery and green pepper and cook for about 5 minutes until softened.

2 Stir in the stock, potatoes, bay leaf and marjoram and bring to the boil. Reduce the heat, cover and simmer for 15–20 minutes or until the potatoes are tender.

3 In a small bowl, blend the flour with 150 ml (¼ pint) of the milk. Whisk the mixture into the chowder and stir until it begins to boil, then slowly add the remaining milk. Season to taste with salt and pepper.

4 Reduce the heat, add the mussels and simmer gently, stirring occasionally, for 5 minutes, without boiling. Stir in the cream, then pour the chowder into a warm soup tureen. Sprinkle the parsley over the top to garnish and serve with crusty French bread.

15
PREP

30
COOK

4
SERVES

rich

2 tablespoons **olive oil**

250 g (8 oz) rindless **smoked streaky bacon**, chopped

2 **onions**, finely chopped

1 **celery stick**, thinly sliced

1 **green pepper**, cored, deseeded and finely chopped

450 ml (¾ pint) **Fish Stock** (see page 16)

250 g (8 oz) **potatoes**, diced

1 **bay leaf**

½ teaspoon chopped **marjoram**

3 tablespoons **plain flour**

300 ml (½ pint) **milk**

500 g (1 lb) cooked shelled **mussels**, thawed if frozen

150 ml (¼ pint) **single cream**

salt and **white pepper**

1 tablespoon finely chopped **parsley**, to garnish

crusty **French bread**, to serve

750 g (1½ lb) **baby clams** or **cockles**, cleaned

3 tablespoons **olive oil**, plus extra to serve

2 large **garlic cloves**, 1 finely chopped and 1 bruised

750 g (1½ lb) **courgettes**, thickly sliced

finely grated rind and juice of 1 **lemon**

1 tablespoon chopped **marjoram**

about 1 litre (1¾ pints) **Vegetable Stock** (see page 19) or **water**

4 thick slices of country **bread**, toasted

salt and **pepper**

15

PREP

25

COOK

4

SERVES

fresh

Clam and courgette soup

In Italy, this light, fresh soup of courgettes and clams is called **aquacotta**, which means 'cooked water'. It is a simple soup, made more substantial by ladling it over toasted bread, as they do in the country.

1 Bring 1 cm (½ inch) water to the boil in a saucepan. Add the clams, cover and steam until they open. Reserve the juice and remove half of the clams from their shells, keeping the remaining clams in their shells. Discard any clams that have not opened.

2 Heat the oil in a large, heavy-based saucepan, add the chopped garlic and cook over a low to moderate heat until golden but not browned. Add the courgettes, lemon rind and marjoram and turn in the oil and garlic. Pour in the stock or water, season lightly with salt and pepper and bring to simmering point. Cover and simmer for 10 minutes or until the courgettes are tender.

3 Pass the soup through a coarse food mill and return to the pan. Add the reserved clam juice, shelled clams and lemon juice. Stir in the clams in their shells and heat through.

4 Rub the toasted bread with the bruised garlic clove and place a slice in each soup bowl. Ladle the soup over the bread, drizzle with olive oil and serve immediately.

Clam chowder

A kilo of clams provides surprisingly little meat, but the pronounced flavour, combined with the salt pork, makes a rich, hearty soup that's good as a starter or, in larger portions, as a main course.

20

PREP

35

COOK

4

SERVES

posh

1 kg (2 lb) **clams**, cleaned

200 g (7 oz) **salt pork**, finely chopped

1 large **onion**, chopped

15 g (½ oz) **butter**

1 tablespoon **plain flour**

4 **tomatoes**, skinned and chopped

350 g (11½ oz) **potatoes**, diced

2 **bay leaves**

3 tablespoons chopped **parsley**

2 teaspoons **Tabasco sauce**

150 ml (¼ pint) **single cream**

1 Bring 150 ml (¼ pint) water to the boil in a saucepan. Add the clams, cover with a tight-fitting lid and cook for 4–5 minutes or until the shells have opened. Drain, reserving the cooking juices, and discard any clams that remain closed. Remove the flesh from the shells and chop it into small pieces.

2 Put the pork and onion in a large saucepan with a knob of the butter and fry gently for 10 minutes or until browned. Stir in the remaining butter until melted. Add the flour and cook, stirring, for 1 minute.

3 Add the clam cooking juices and 450 ml (¾ pint) water, the tomatoes, potatoes and bay leaves. Bring just to the boil, then reduce the heat, cover and cook very gently for 15 minutes or until the potatoes are tender.

4 Stir in the clams and parsley and cook very gently for 2 minutes. Add the Tabasco sauce and cream, heat through and serve.

2 tablespoons **olive oil**

2 **onions**, chopped

2 **celery sticks**, sliced

1 litre (1¾ pints) **Fish Stock** (see page 16)

325 g (11 oz) **potatoes**, cut into small cubes

300 g (10 oz) frozen **sweetcorn kernels**

150 g (5 oz) frozen cooked peeled **prawns**

1 tablespoon chopped **thyme**, **parsley** or fresh **coriander** (optional)

salt and **pepper**

crusty **bread**, to serve

10

PREP

25

COOK

4

SERVES

easy

Sweetcorn and prawn chowder

The three main ingredients in this dish – sweetcorn, frozen prawns and potatoes – are found in most kitchens' emergency reserves. Frozen sweetcorn kernels are preferable to canned sweetcorn kernels, which have a salty, preserved taste.

1 Heat the oil in a large, heavy-based saucepan, add the onions and celery and cook over a moderate heat for 5 minutes.

2 Add the stock and bring to the boil. Reduce the heat and add the potatoes. Cover and simmer gently for 8–10 minutes.

3 Add the sweetcorn kernels and cook for 5 minutes, then add the prawns and herbs (if using). Cook gently for a further 2–3 minutes to heat through. Season to taste with salt and pepper and ladle into warm soup bowls.

Prawn soup with okra

Okra is used extensively in Creole cuisine. It looks a little like a small courgette and adds colour and texture to dishes. These days you should be able to buy it quite easily in most large supermarkets.

1 Melt the butter in a large, heavy-based saucepan and add the onion and celery. Cover and cook over a moderate heat until the onion starts to soften but not brown. Add the stock and rice, cover and cook over a low heat for 20 minutes or until the rice is tender.

2 Prepare the okra by cutting away the conical cap from the stalk end, then cutting the okra into 1 cm (½ inch) slices.

3 Add the okra, tomatoes, prawns and ham to the soup and cook, stirring frequently, for a further 5–8 minutes. Spoon the soup into warm soup bowls and garnish generously with small parsley leaves.

15
PREP

35
COOK

4
SERVES

exotic

50 g (2 oz) **butter**

1 **onion**, finely chopped

200 g (7 oz) **celery sticks**, thinly sliced

1 litre (1¾ pints) **Fish Stock** (see page 16)

50 g (2 oz) **white long-grain rice**

250 g (8 oz) **okra**

2 **tomatoes**, skinned and finely chopped

250 g (8 oz) cooked peeled **prawns**, thawed if frozen

50 g (2 oz) cooked **ham**, cut into fine strips

small **parsley leaves**, to garnish

50 g (2 oz) **butter**

2 **garlic cloves**, crushed

1 **onion**, chopped

1 **red pepper**, cored,
deseeded and finely
chopped

4 ripe **tomatoes**, skinned
and chopped

¼ teaspoon **cayenne
pepper** (or to taste)

1.2 litres (2 pints) **Fish
Stock** (see page 16)

375 g (12 oz) **okra,**
trimmed and sliced

375 g (12 oz) cooked
peeled **prawns**, thawed if
frozen

50 g (2 oz) cooked
white long-grain rice

1 tablespoon **lime juice**

salt and **pepper**

20

PREP

40

COOK

4

SERVES

spicy

Prawn gumbo

This Cajun gumbo is a traditional dish along
the Louisiana coast. Gumbo can be made with
a variety of vegetables, meats and seafood,
but okra is the most important ingredient.
The soup can be made 24 hours in advance
and kept, covered, in the refrigerator.

1 Melt the butter in a large heavy-based
saucepan, add the garlic and onion and cook
over a moderate heat for about 5 minutes or
until softened.

2 Add the red pepper to the pan and cook for
5 minutes. Stir in the tomatoes and cayenne
pepper and mix well. Pour in the stock and
bring to the boil. Stir in the okra. Reduce the
heat, cover and cook, stirring occasionally,
for 20 minutes.

3 Add the prawns, rice and lime juice to the
soup, then stir well. Cover and simmer for a
further 5–8 minutes. Season to taste with salt
and pepper and add a little more cayenne
pepper, if liked. Serve immediately in warm
soup bowls.

Simple prawn bisque

This recipe really is as simple as its name suggests. You can buy ready peeled prawns or, if you have the time and inclination, buy them whole and peel them yourself.

1 Melt the butter in a large, heavy-based saucepan, add the onion, carrot and celery and cook over a moderate heat for 5 minutes or until softened.

2 Reserve 125 g (4 oz) of the prawns. Add the remaining prawns to the pan with the tomatoes, stock, sherry, bay leaf, nutmeg and potatoes. Season to taste with pepper. Bring to simmering point, then reduce the heat, cover and cook for 25–30 minutes or until all the vegetables are tender. Remove and discard the bay leaf.

3 In a blender or food processor, blend the soup in batches, and transfer it to a clean saucepan. Add the reserved prawns, season to taste with salt and reheat gently. Just before serving, stir in the cream and sprinkle with the parsley or chives to garnish.

15 PREP

40 COOK

6 SERVES

simple

50 g (2 oz) **butter**

1 small **onion**, finely chopped

1 **carrot**, finely chopped

1 **celery stick**, thinly sliced

500 g (1 lb) cooked peeled **prawns**, thawed if frozen

400 g (13 oz) can chopped **tomatoes**

900 ml (1½ pints) **Fish Stock** (see page 16)

1 tablespoon **medium dry sherry**

1 **bay leaf**

pinch of **grated nutmeg**

250 g (8 oz) **potatoes**, thinly sliced

125 ml (4 fl oz) **double cream**

salt and **pepper**

1 tablespoon finely chopped **parsley** or snipped **chives**, to garnish

50 g (2 oz) **butter**

2 **fennel bulbs**, trimmed and finely sliced, fronds reserved to garnish

600 ml (1 pint) **Fish Stock** (see page 16)

600 ml (1 pint) **milk**

¼ teaspoon **white pepper**

300 g (10 oz) **potatoes**, diced

175 g (6 oz) cooked peeled **prawns**, thawed if frozen

150 ml (¼ pint) **single cream**

salt

PREP
15

25
COOK

4
SERVES

stylish

Prawn and fennel soup

This soup doesn't need many ingredients because prawns and fennel are such wonderfully unique flavours that can hold their own. The subtle aniseed taste of fennel is mellowed by the addition of milk and cream.

1 Melt the butter in a large, heavy-based saucepan and add the sliced fennel. Cover tightly and cook over a moderate heat, stirring occasionally, for 5 minutes or until beginning to soften.

2 Add the stock, milk, pepper and potatoes and bring to simmering point. Reduce the heat, cover and simmer gently for 15–20 minutes or until the vegetables are tender.

3 In a blender or food processor, blend the soup in batches, then transfer it to a clean saucepan. Add the prawns, season to taste with salt and stir in the cream. Reheat gently without boiling. Spoon into warm soup bowls and garnish with a sprinkling of finely chopped fennel fronds.

Cream of celery and prawn soup

This wonderfully creamy soup can be served chilled. It would make a great dinner party starter because you can prepare the whole dish in advance and leave it chilling in the refrigerator until you are ready to serve.

5*

PREP

10

COOK

3

SERVES

quick

300 g (10 oz) can **condensed cream of celery soup**

300 ml (½ pint) **milk**

1 teaspoon **paprika**

½ teaspoon **white pepper**

2 tablespoons **natural yogurt**

150 g (5 oz) cooked peeled **prawns**, thawed if frozen

snipped **chives**, to garnish

1 Mix together the soup and milk in a large, heavy-based saucepan. Add the paprika and pepper. Bring to simmering point and cook, stirring constantly, for 5 minutes. Remove from the heat.

2 If serving the soup hot, stir in the yogurt and prawns and gently heat through for about 2 minutes without boiling. Spoon into warm soup bowls, garnish each portion with snipped chives and serve immediately.

3 If serving the soup chilled, pour the soup into a bowl and leave to cool. Stir in the yogurt and prawns, cover and chill in the refrigerator for at least 3 hours. Serve the soup in chilled bowls, each portion garnished with snipped chives.

* Plus 3 hours chilling if served cold

5 **red bird's eye chillies**

6 **kaffir lime leaves**

1 string of **green peppercorns**

1 **lemon grass stalk**, finely sliced

900 ml (1½ pints) **water**

2 tablespoons **Thai fish sauce**

2 teaspoons **caster sugar**

500 g (1 lb) raw peeled and deveined **tiger prawns**

4 tablespoons **kaffir lime juice**

handful of fresh **coriander**

plain boiled rice, to serve

10

PREP

15

COOK

4

SERVES

exotic

Prawn and kaffir lime soup

Strings of green peppercorns can be found in Asian stores. They are added to Thai and Cambodian curries to add a peppery flavour, but are not eaten. If you cannot find them, use peppercorns in brine and tie 1 tablespoon of the drained peppercorns in a piece of muslin. Discard before eating.

1 Put the chillies, kaffir lime leaves, peppercorns, lemon grass and measured water in a large, heavy-based saucepan and slowly bring to the boil. Boil for 10 minutes.

2 Reduce the heat and add the fish sauce and sugar. When the liquid is simmering, add the prawns and simmer gently for 2–3 minutes or until they have turned pink. Remove the pan from the heat and add the lime juice and coriander. Serve immediately in warm bowls with plain boiled rice.

Crab and rice soup

15
PREP

Crab has a wonderfully rich, distinctive taste that takes well to other flavours, such as saffron. Although real saffron is expensive, you only a couple of threads to make a big difference to the flavour and colour of a dish.

80
COOK

6
SERVES

posh

1 Heat the oil in a large, heavy-based saucepan, add the crab meat and cook over a moderate heat, stirring frequently, until lightly browned. Add the onion and cook, stirring constantly, for 5 minutes. Add the tomatoes, paprika, salt and measured boiling water. Cover and simmer gently for about 45 minutes.

2 Meanwhile, pound the garlic with a pinch of salt and the parsley sprigs in a mortar with a pestle. Add the saffron and 2 tablespoons of the simmering stock. Stir well.

3 Add the rice and the garlic mixture to the pan. Partially cover and simmer for 20 minutes or until the rice is tender. Remove the pan from the heat and leave the soup to rest for 2–3 minutes. Stir, then taste and adjust the seasoning if necessary. Pour the soup into a warm tureen and serve hot with croûtons, if liked.

4 tablespoons **olive oil**

500 g (1 lb) **white crab meat**, cut into 1 cm (½ inch) pieces

1 **onion**, chopped

250 g (8 oz) **tomatoes**, skinned and chopped

1 teaspoon **paprika**

½ teaspoon **salt** (or to taste)

1.8 litres (3 pints) boiling **water**

2 **garlic cloves**

2 sprigs of **parsley**, leaves stripped from the stalks

2 **saffron threads**

250 g (8 oz) **white long-grain rice**

croûtons, to garnish (optional)

300 g (10 oz) can **condensed cream of tomato soup**

300 ml (½ pint) **milk**

175 g (6 oz) can **white crab meat** in brine

½ teaspoon **mild curry powder**

1 teaspoon **Worcestershire sauce**

2 teaspoons **medium dry sherry**

2 tablespoons **double cream**

snipped **chives** or finely chopped **parsley**, to garnish (optional)

croûtons, to serve (optional)

5

PREP

10

COOK

4

SERVES

easy

Crab meat bisque

This is such a quick and easy soup that you can make it for lunch or dinner even if you are short of time. Make sure you have all the ingredients ready before you begin cooking.

1 Mix the soup and milk in a large, heavy-based saucepan. Bring to simmering point and cook, stirring constantly, for 3 minutes. Add the crab meat with the brine, then stir in the curry powder, Worcestershire sauce and sherry. Cook, stirring, for a further 3 minutes or until almost boiling.

2 Remove the pan from the heat and stir in the cream. Spoon the soup into warm soup bowls, garnish each portion with snipped chives or finely chopped parsley, if liked, and serve immediately. If the bisque is intended to be more substantial, serve with croûtons.

Sweetcorn soup with crab meat

Ginger works well with the oriental theme of this recipe. To prepare, simply cut a large piece and carefully slice off the skin. Use a cheese grater to grate the required amount, turning the piece of ginger as you grate so that it doesn't become stringy.

15

PREP

20

COOK

4

SERVES

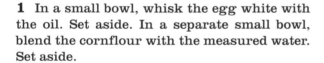

light

1 In a small bowl, whisk the egg white with the oil. Set aside. In a separate small bowl, blend the cornflour with the measured water. Set aside.

2 Bring the stock to the boil in a large, heavy-based saucepan. Add the sweetcorn kernels, reduce the heat and simmer for 10 minutes. Add the sherry, ginger, salt and sugar. Stir in the reserved cornflour mixture. Bring to the boil, stirring, then reduce the heat and simmer, stirring frequently, for 3–5 minutes.

3 Add the crab meat to the pan and stir well. Cook for 2 minutes. Pour in the reserved egg white mixture slowly and in a steady stream, stirring constantly. Ladle the soup into a warm tureen, sprinkle with the spring onion tops to garnish and serve immediately.

1 **egg white**

1 teaspoon **sesame oil**

2 teaspoons **cornflour**

2 teaspoons **water**

1.2 litres (2 pints) **Chicken Stock** (see page 17)

275 g (9 oz) can **sweetcorn kernels**, drained

2 tablespoons **dry sherry**

2 teaspoons grated fresh **root ginger**

½ teaspoon **salt**

1 teaspoon **caster sugar**

175 g (6 oz) can **white crab meat** in brine, drained

2 tablespoons finely chopped **spring onion tops**, to garnish

25 g (1 oz) **butter**

1 tablespoon **sunflower oil**

1 **onion**, chopped

1 **baking potato**, diced

600 ml (1 pint) semi-skimmed **milk**

1 **fish stock cube**, crumbled

2 **bay leaves**

grated nutmeg

1 fillet of undyed **smoked haddock**, about 250 g (8 oz), cut in half

125 g (4 oz) **baby spinach**, stalks discarded, torn into pieces

salt and **pepper**

4 grilled rashers of rindless **streaky bacon**, to garnish (optional)

15

PREP

25

COOK

3

SERVES

filling

Haddock and spinach chowder

American-style chowders feature among the easiest soups to prepare because the fish and vegetables are simply poached in milk and left in their chunky form, resulting in a creamy, satisfying soup.

1 Melt the butter with the oil in a large, heavy-based saucepan, add the onion and cook over a moderate heat for 5 minutes or until softened but not browned. Add the potato and cook, stirring frequently, for about 5 minutes or until lightly browned.

2 Stir in the milk, stock cube, bay leaves and nutmeg. Season to taste with salt and pepper. Add the haddock and bring to the boil. Reduce the heat, cover and simmer for 10 minutes or until the haddock flakes easily. Using a slotted spoon, transfer the haddock to a plate and leave to cool. Remove and discard the skin and flake the flesh into pieces, carefully removing and discarding any remaining bones.

3 Add the spinach to the pan and cook for 2–3 minutes or until tender. Add the haddock and reheat gently.

4 Cut the grilled bacon into strips (if using). Ladle the soup into warm soup bowls and garnish with the bacon.

Haddock and sweetcorn chowder

Smoked haddock has real depth of flavour, and it combines here to perfect effect with sweetcorn kernels and milk to produce a rich, thick soup that's delicious served with fresh crusty bread.

15

PREP

25

COOK

4

SERVES

rich

1 large **potato**, diced

1 **bay leaf**

300 ml (½ pint) **milk**

600 ml (1 pint) **water**

250–300 g (8–10 oz) skinned **smoked haddock** fillet, roughly chopped, with any remaining bones removed

200 g (7 oz) can **sweetcorn kernels**, drained

3 tablespoons frozen **peas**

1½ tablespoons **cornflour**

¼ teaspoon **paprika**

½ teaspoon **white pepper**

salt (optional)

2 tablespoons finely chopped **parsley**

1 Put the potato and bay leaf in a large, heavy-based saucepan. Add the milk and measured water and bring to the boil. Reduce the heat and simmer for 5 minutes or until the potato is almost tender.

2 Add the haddock, cover and simmer for 10 minutes. Add the sweetcorn kernels and peas and simmer for a further 5 minutes. Remove and discard the bay leaf.

3 In a small bowl, blend the cornflour, paprika and pepper with 3–4 tablespoons of the soup liquid. Add the cornflour mixture to the pan and cook, stirring constantly, for 5 minutes or until the soup has thickened. Taste and add salt if necessary, then stir in the parsley. Serve the soup immediately in warm soup bowls.

25 g (1 oz) **butter**

250 g (8 oz) **fennel bulbs**, trimmed and finely sliced, fronds reserved to garnish

1 **leek**, white part only, sliced

600 ml (1 pint) **Fish Stock** (see page 16)

1 **bay leaf**

300 g (10 oz) **potatoes**, thinly sliced

250 g (8 oz) skinned **haddock** fillet

300 ml (½ pint) **milk**

½ teaspoon **white pepper**

salt

PREP

COOK

SERVES

tasty

Haddock and fennel soup

The slight aniseed flavour of fennel enhances most fish soups. Its feathery fronds can be finely chopped and sprinkled over the soup as a garnish.

1 Melt the butter in a large, heavy-based saucepan, add the sliced fennel and leek and cook for 5 minutes or until softened. Add the stock, bay leaf and potatoes and bring to the boil. Reduce the heat, cover and simmer for 10–15 minutes or until all the vegetables are tender. Remove and discard the bay leaf.

2 Meanwhile, in a separate saucepan, mix together the haddock, milk and pepper and bring to the boil. Reduce the heat, cover and simmer for 5 minutes. Remove the pan from the heat and leave to stand, covered, for 5 minutes. Break the fish into large flakes.

3 In a blender or food processor, blend 300 ml (½ pint) of the vegetable and stock mixture until smooth. Return to the pan and add the haddock and milk mixture. Stir well and heat through without boiling. Serve the soup in warm soup bowls, garnished with finely chopped fennel fronds.

Smoked haddock and corn soup

Wild rice isn't actually rice; it's a grain that's grown in marshes. It adds an unusual nutty taste that is complemented by the saltiness of the smoked haddock.

15
PREP

90
COOK

4
SERVES

thick

75 g (3 oz) **wild rice**

250 g (8 oz) **smoked haddock**

600 ml (1 pint) **milk**

1 **bay leaf**

50 g (2 oz) **butter**

1 large **onion**, chopped

1 **leek**, trimmed, cleaned and sliced

1 **celery stick**, chopped

1 **garlic clove**, crushed

1 tablespoon **thyme** leaves

900 ml (1½ pints) **Chicken Stock** (see page 17)

pinch of **grated nutmeg**

125 g (4 oz) **sweetcorn kernels**, thawed if frozen

salt and **pepper**

2 tablespoons chopped **parsley**, to garnish

1 Put the rice in a saucepan and cover with water. Bring to the boil. Reduce the heat and simmer for 40–45 minutes until tender. Drain.

2 Put the haddock, milk and bay leaf in a large, heavy-based saucepan and bring to the boil. Reduce the heat and simmer for 8–10 minutes until just cooked. Using a slotted spoon, transfer the haddock to a plate and leave to cool. Remove and discard the skin and flake the flesh into pieces, carefully removing and discarding any bones. Strain the milk through a sieve and reserve.

3 Melt the butter in a clean, large, heavy-based saucepan, add the onion, leek, celery and garlic and cook over a low heat, stirring frequently, for 8–10 minutes until softened but not browned. Add the thyme, stock, reserved milk, nutmeg and salt and pepper to taste. Bring to the boil. Reduce the heat and simmer for 10 minutes. Add the sweetcorn and simmer for 5 minutes. Add the rice and haddock and simmer for 5 minutes. Serve in warm soup bowls, sprinkled with the parsley.

50 g (2 oz) **butter**

250 g (8 oz) **celery sticks**, thinly sliced, leaves reserved to garnish

1 **leek**, white part only, sliced

600 ml (1 pint) **Fish Stock** (see page 16)

1 **bay leaf**

300 g (10 oz) **potatoes**, thinly sliced

250 g (8 oz) skinned **cod** fillet

300 ml (½ pint) **milk**

½ teaspoon **white pepper**

salt

PREP

COOK

SERVES

simple

Cod and celery soup

This variation on Haddock and Fennel Soup (see page 66) is an ideal alternative for people who do not like the aniseed taste of fennel.

1 Melt the butter in a large, heavy-based saucepan, add the celery and leek and cook for 5 minutes or until softened. Add the stock, bay leaf and potatoes and bring to the boil. Reduce the heat, cover and simmer for 10–15 minutes or until all the vegetables are tender. Remove and discard the bay leaf.

2 Meanwhile, in a separate saucepan, mix together the cod, milk and pepper and bring to the boil. Reduce the heat, cover and simmer for 5 minutes. Remove from the heat and leave to stand, covered, for 5 minutes. Break the fish into large flakes.

3 In a blender or food processor, blend 300 ml (½ pint) of the vegetable and stock mixture until smooth. Return to the pan and add the cod and milk mixture. Stir well and heat through without boiling. Serve the soup in warm soup bowls, garnished with finely chopped celery leaves.

Cod soup with rice and tomatoes

Although you probably wouldn't want to eat a fish head, they are fantastic for adding flavour to soups and fish stock. In this recipe, it will help to enhance the taste of the cod.

20
PREP

90
COOK

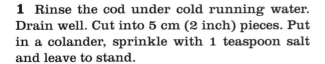

4
SERVES

tasty

1 Rinse the cod under cold running water. Drain well. Cut into 5 cm (2 inch) pieces. Put in a colander, sprinkle with 1 teaspoon salt and leave to stand.

2 Put all the vegetables, parsley and fish head in a large, heavy-based saucepan. Add the measured water and season to taste with salt and pepper. Bring to the boil, then reduce the heat and simmer for 45 minutes. Remove and discard the fish head and parsley.

3 Rinse the cod pieces again under cold running water, add to the pan and cook over a moderate heat for 15–20 minutes or until cooked but still firm. Using a slotted spoon, transfer the cod pieces to a dish, cover and keep hot. Slowly pour the oil into the soup, then add the rice. Partially cover and cook over a moderate heat for 25 minutes or until the rice is tender. Return the cod pieces to the soup and gently heat through. Taste and adjust the seasoning if necessary, then serve immediately in warm soup bowls.

750 g (1½ lb) **cod**, skinned and boned

4 large **tomatoes**, skinned and roughly chopped

2 large **onions**, thinly sliced

2 **celery sticks**, thinly sliced

4 sprigs of **parsley**

1 **fish head**

1.8 litres (3 pints) **water**

5 tablespoons **olive oil**

50 g (2 oz) **white short-grain rice**

salt and **pepper**

Kipper soup

15

PREP

20

COOK

6

SERVES

easy

375 g (12 oz) **kipper** fillet

600 ml (1 pint) **water**

2 x 425 g (14 oz) cans **plum tomatoes**

1 tablespoon **tomato purée**

1½ tablespoons **cornflour**

1 teaspoon **lemon juice**

1 tablespoon **Worcestershire sauce**

¼ teaspoon **celery salt**

cayenne pepper

TO GARNISH:

3 tablespoons **soured cream** (optional)

2 tablespoons snipped **chives**

Kippers are often eaten only at breakfast, so it's good to see them used in this piquant soup. These cured herrings are a natural partner for tomatoes, and the cayenne pepper and Worcestershire sauce add a bit of a kick.

1 Put the kippers in a large, heavy-based saucepan and add the measured water. Bring to simmering point, then reduce the heat, cover tightly and cook for 5 minutes. Drain, reserving 450 ml (¾ pint) of the liquid.

2 Remove and discard the skin from the kippers and flake the flesh into pieces. In a blender or food processor, blend the fish with the tomatoes, tomato purée and 300 ml (½ pint) of the reserved liquid. Transfer the mixture to a clean saucepan.

3 In a small bowl, blend the cornflour with the remaining liquid. Stir the cornflour mixture into the pan and add the lemon juice, Worcestershire sauce and celery salt, with cayenne pepper to taste. Simmer, stirring, for 5–8 minutes or until the soup thickens slightly. Spoon into warm soup bowls, garnish each portion with a swirl of soured cream, if liked, and a generous sprinkling of snipped chives and serve immediately.

Tuna and red pepper chowder

You can use fresh, cooked tuna steak for this recipe, if you prefer. The sweetcorn kernels, red pepper and parsley make for a colourful finished dish.

1 Melt the butter in a large, heavy-based saucepan and add the red pepper and celery. Cover and cook over a moderate heat, stirring frequently, for 8–10 minutes. When the mixture becomes a little dry, moisten it with the wine.

2 Add the stock, potatoes and marjoram, partially cover and simmer for 15 minutes.

3 Stir in the sweetcorn kernels and tuna, season to taste with salt and pepper and simmer gently, uncovered, for a further 10 minutes. Stir in the parsley, then serve the chowder immediately in warm bowls, with crusty French bread, if liked.

15
PREP

35
COOK

4

SERVES

herby

50 g (2 oz) **butter**

1 small **red pepper**, cored, deseeded and chopped

1 **celery stick**, thinly sliced

1 tablespoon **dry white wine**

1.2 litres (2 pints) **Fish Stock** (see page 16)

250 g (8 oz) **potatoes**, cut into 1 cm (½ inch) cubes

1 teaspoon finely chopped **marjoram**

340 g (11½ oz) can **sweetcorn kernels**, drained

200 g (7 oz) can **tuna chunks** in brine, drained and shredded

2 tablespoons finely chopped **parsley**

salt and **pepper**

crusty French **bread**, to serve (optional)

1 kg (2 lb) **mussels** and **clams**, scrubbed and debearded

500 g (1 lb) **small squid**, cleaned, tentacles removed and sliced into rings

500 g (1 lb) raw medium or large peeled and deveined **prawns**

1.75 kg (3½ lb) **whole mixed fish**, cleaned

BROTH:

150 ml (¼ pint) extra virgin **olive oil**

4 **leeks**, sliced

4 **garlic cloves**, finely chopped

300 ml (½ pint) **dry white wine**

pinch of **saffron threads**

750 g (1½ lb) ripe **plum tomatoes**, roughly chopped

6 **sun-dried tomatoes in oil**, drained and roughly chopped

1 teaspoon **fennel seeds**

1 tablespoon **dried oregano**

600 ml (1 pint) **water**

30

PREP

45

COOK

6

SERVES

rich

Sicilian fish soup

In coastal areas of Sicily, piles of mixed small fish are especially set aside for fish soup, and there will also be squid, shellfish and large prawns. A well-flavoured broth is made with saffron and fennel seeds, and the seafood is poached in it. Traditionally, the fish is served first and the broth is ladled on top.

1 Make the broth. Heat the oil in a large, deep, flameproof casserole, add the leeks and garlic and cook over a moderate heat for 5 minutes or until the leeks are softened. Add the wine and boil until reduced by half. Add the saffron, tomatoes, fennel seeds, oregano and measured water and bring to the boil. Reduce the heat, cover and simmer for 20 minutes until the tomatoes and oil separate.

2 Put the mussels and clams in a bowl of cold water. Add the squid to the casserole and poach for 3–4 minutes. Remove with a slotted spoon, cover and keep warm. Add the prawns and simmer until opaque and cooked. Remove with a slotted spoon and keep warm.

3 Drain the mussels and clams and add to the broth. Cover and cook for a few minutes until they open. Remove with a slotted spoon and keep warm, discarding any that have not opened. Poach the remaining fish until just cooked, then remove from the broth. Arrange the fish on a serving dish with the shellfish and squid on top. Moisten the fish with some of the broth and serve the rest separately.

Seafood soup

Many Spanish dishes can be identified by the presence of nuts, which are used to flavour and thicken sauces. The seafood in this recipe can be varied to suit individual tastes, for example substituting langoustines for the lobsters, or cod for the monkfish.

1 Soak the saffron in the boiling stock for 10 minutes. Meanwhile, heat half of the oil in a large, flameproof casserole, add the onion, garlic, thyme and chilli flakes and cook over a moderate heat for 10 minutes or until the onion is lightly golden. Pour in the sherry and boil until reduced by half, then add the tomatoes, stock and a little salt and pepper. Bring to the boil, then reduce the heat, cover and simmer for 20 minutes. Transfer 150 ml (¼ pint) of the broth to a bowl and reserve.

2 Discard the lobster heads, cut the bodies in half lengthways and separate the claws. Cut the monkfish into cubes and dust lightly with the flour. Scrub and debeard the mussels and scrub the clams. Add all the seafood to the casserole and return to the boil, stirring well. Cover and simmer for a further 10 minutes or until all the seafood is cooked.

3 Combine the ground almonds, vinegar, remaining oil and reserved broth and stir into the stew. Cook, stirring, for 5 minutes until thickened. Serve in warm soup bowls with crusty bread, accompanied by finger bowls.

30*
PREP

50
COOK

4
SERVES

posh

* Plus 10 minutes soaking

few **saffron threads**

150 ml (¼ pint) boiling **Fish Stock** (see page 16)

4 tablespoons **olive oil**

1 **onion**, chopped

2 **garlic cloves**, crushed

1 tablespoon chopped **thyme**

¼ teaspoon dried **chilli flakes**

100 ml (3½ fl oz) **dry sherry**

400 g (13 oz) can chopped **tomatoes**

2 small cooked **lobsters**, each about 475 g (15 oz)

500 g (1 lb) **monkfish** fillet

2 tablespoons **plain flour**

12 large raw peeled and deveined **prawns**

500 g (1 lb) **mussels**

500 g (1 lb) **clams**

50 g (2 oz) ground **toasted almonds**

1 tablespoon **sherry vinegar**

salt and **pepper**

crusty **bread**, to serve

4 tablespoons **olive oil**

2 **garlic cloves**, finely chopped

2 **onions**, chopped

500 g (1 lb) prepared **mackerel**, cut into bite-sized pieces

500 g (1 lb) **whiting** fillet, cut into bite-sized pieces

500 g (1 lb) **haddock** or **cod** fillet, cut into bite-sized pieces

250 g (8 oz) raw peeled **prawns**

6 **tomatoes**, skinned and chopped

½ teaspoon **saffron threads**

1.5 litres (2½ pints) hot **Fish Stock** (see page 16)

1 **bay leaf**

3 sprigs of **parsley**

10–12 **mussels**, scrubbed and debearded

6–8 slices **French bread**

salt and **pepper**

2 tablespoons finely chopped **parsley**, to garnish

35

PREP

40

COOK

6

SERVES

classic

Bouillabaisse

This is another classic dish that is somewhere between a soup and a stew because of its chunky consistency and hearty ingredients. The fish will be lovely and tender, and will soak up some of the wonderful juices.

1 Heat the oil in a large, heavy-based saucepan and add the garlic and onions. Cover and cook over a moderate heat for 5 minutes or until the onions are softened but not browned. Add the mackerel, whiting, haddock or cod and cook, uncovered and stirring occasionally, for 10 minutes.

2 Add the prawns and tomatoes. Dissolve the saffron in the boiling stock and add to the pan with the bay leaf, parsley sprigs and salt and pepper to taste. Stir and bring to the boil. Reduce the heat, cover and simmer for 15 minutes. Add the mussels and cook for a further 10 minutes or until the fish is cooked.

3 Remove and discard the bay leaf, parsley and any mussels that have not opened. Place the bread in a warm soup tureen and ladle in the soup. Sprinkle with the chopped parsley before serving.

Philippine sour fish soup

20 PREP

30 COOK

4 SERVES

exotic

In the Philippines, star fruit, or carambolas, are included in soups and meat dishes for their slightly tart flavour. This soup, known as **sinaging**, is usually served with plain boiled rice.

1 Put the onion, garlic, tomatoes, star fruit, lemon juice and measured water in a large, heavy-based saucepan and bring to a fast simmer. Cover and simmer for 20 minutes.

2 Add the fish sauce to the pan and, with the back of a wooden spoon, break up the star fruit pieces into a pulp. Add the fish and simmer gently for 8–10 minutes.

3 Taste the soup and season with salt and pepper if necessary. Serve in large, warm soup bowls with extra fish sauce, lime wedges and pickled green chillies.

1 **onion**, finely chopped

2 **garlic cloves**, crushed

500 g (1 lb) unripe **tomatoes**, quartered

1 **star fruit**, thickly sliced

4 tablespoons **lemon juice**

1.2 litres (2 pints) **water**

3 tablespoons **Thai fish sauce**, plus extra to serve

750 g (1½ lb) **mixed white fish**

salt and **pepper**

TO SERVE:

lime wedges

pickled green chillies

vegetables

1 tablespoon **sunflower oil**

1 kg (2 lb) **pumpkin**, peeled, deseeded and cut into 2.5 cm (1 inch) cubes

1 **onion**, chopped

250 g (8 oz) **carrots**, diced

1 **celery stick**, sliced

2 teaspoons **curry powder**

1 tablespoon **wholewheat flour**

1.2 litres (2 pints) **Chicken Stock** (see page 17)

250 g (8 oz) **bacon**, trimmed of fat and diced

salt and **pepper**

TO GARNISH:

pumpkin seeds

grated nutmeg

15

PREP

20

COOK

6

SERVES

tasty

Tuscan pumpkin soup

This quick soup is perfect for a nourishing midweek supper. Pumpkin is becoming more widely popular and rightly so – it's a versatile vegetable that's very nutritious, too.

1 Heat the oil in a large, heavy-based saucepan, add the pumpkin, onion, carrots and celery and cook over a moderate heat for 5 minutes or until lightly browned. Stir in the curry powder and cook for a further 1 minute. Stir in the flour. Remove from the heat and stir in the stock.

2 In a blender or food processor, blend the soup in batches until smooth, then return it to the pan.

3 Heat a dry nonstick frying pan, add the bacon and cook over a moderate to high heat, stirring constantly, for 3–4 minutes. Remove with a slotted spoon and drain on kitchen paper, then add to the soup. Taste and adjust the seasoning if necessary, then bring the soup to the boil. Reduce the heat and simmer, stirring, for 5 minutes.

4 Spoon the soup into warm soup bowls, garnish with pumpkin seeds and nutmeg and serve immediately.

Pumpkin and coconut soup

Coconut milk isn't the liquid you find inside the coconut – that's coconut water. The milk is produced by squeezing the flesh of the coconut, which produces a much thicker and creamier liquid than the water. To make a more substantial dish, serve with naan bread.

1 Heat the oil in a large, heavy-based saucepan, add the onion, garlic, ginger, chillies and spices and cook over a moderate heat, stirring frequently, for 10 minutes.

2 Add the pumpkin, stock, coconut milk, tamarind pulp and cinnamon stick and bring to the boil. Reduce the heat, cover and simmer gently for 10 minutes, or until the pumpkin is just tender.

3 Remove and discard the cinnamon stick. In a blender or food processor, blend the soup with the fresh coriander until smooth. Transfer the soup to warm soup bowls and serve immediately, garnished with coriander leaves and yogurt.

15 PREP

25 COOK

4 SERVES

spicy

2 tablespoons **sunflower oil**

1 **onion**, chopped

4 **garlic cloves**, crushed

2.5 cm (1 inch) piece of fresh **root ginger**, peeled and grated

2 **red chillies**, deseeded and chopped

1 teaspoon **ground coriander**

½ teaspoon **ground cumin**

seeds from 2 **cardamom pods**

750 g (1½ lb) **pumpkin**, peeled, deseeded and diced

750 ml (1¼ pints) **Vegetable Stock** (see page 19)

150 ml (¼ pint) **coconut milk**

1 tablespoon **tamarind pulp**

1 **cinnamon stick**

2 tablespoons chopped fresh **coriander**, plus extra to garnish

salt and **pepper**

natural yogurt, to garnish

750 g (1½ lb) **pumpkin**, peeled, deseeded and cut into large cubes

6 **garlic cloves**, unpeeled

4 tablespoons **olive oil**

2 **onions**, thinly sliced

2 **celery sticks**, chopped

50 g (2 oz) **white long-grain rice**

1.5 litres (2½ pints) **Vegetable Stock** (see page 19) or **water**

4 tablespoons chopped **parsley**

salt and **pepper**

15

PREP

45

COOK

6

SERVES

thick

Pumpkin and garlic soup

Roasting the pumpkin and garlic together concentrates the flavour of the pumpkin, which can be bland. Look for a variety of pumpkin with bright orange flesh, or try using butternut squash instead.

1 Put the pumpkin in a roasting tin with the garlic and toss with half of the oil. Roast in a preheated oven, 200°C (400°F), Gas Mark 6, for 30 minutes or until very tender and beginning to brown.

2 Meanwhile, heat the remaining oil in a large, heavy-based saucepan, add the onions and celery and cook over a low heat for 10 minutes or until just beginning to brown. Stir in the rice and stock or water and bring to the boil. Reduce the heat, cover and simmer for 15–20 minutes or until the rice is tender.

3 Remove the pumpkin and garlic from the oven and leave to cool slightly. Pop the garlic cloves out of their skins and add to the pan with the pumpkin. Bring to the boil, then reduce the heat and simmer for 10 minutes.

4 In a blender or food processor, roughly blend the soup in batches, then return it to the pan. Season to taste with salt and pepper. Add a little more stock or water if the soup is too thick. Reheat gently, then stir in the parsley and serve immediately in warm bowls.

Pumpkin soup with coriander pistou

Coriander is used in the pistou (the French word for pesto), replacing the more familiar basil, and adding a North African influence to this Provençal soup.

20

PREP

35

COOK

6

SERVES

herby

1 Arrange the pumpkin, thyme and garlic in a roasting tin so that they fit snugly in a single layer. Add half of the oil and toss gently to coat. Season to taste with salt and pepper. Roast in a preheated oven, 200°C (400°F), Gas Mark 6, for 30 minutes or until charred and tender.

2 Meanwhile, heat the remaining oil in a large, heavy-based saucepan, add the onion, celery and chilli and cook over a low heat for 10 minutes or until softened. Add the stock and bring to the boil. Reduce the heat, cover and simmer for 20 minutes. Stir in the roasted pumpkin and return to the boil, then reduce the heat and simmer for 5 minutes.

3 Remove and discard the thyme. In a blender or food processor, blend the soup in batches until really smooth. Keep warm.

4 Put all the ingredients for the pistou in a spice grinder and grind to a smooth paste or use a pestle and mortar. Spoon the soup into warm soup bowls and swirl a little pistou into each one just before serving.

500 g (1 lb) **pumpkin** flesh, cut into cubes

4 sprigs of **thyme**

4 **garlic cloves**, peeled but left whole

4 tablespoons **olive oil**

1 **onion**, chopped

2 **celery sticks**, sliced

1 **red chilli**, deseeded and chopped

1.2 litres (2 pints) **Vegetable Stock** (see page 19)

salt and **pepper**

CORIANDER PISTOU:

25 g (1 oz) fresh **coriander**

1 **garlic clove**, crushed

1 tablespoon **blanched almonds**, chopped

4 tablespoons extra virgin **olive oil**

1 tablespoon grated **Parmesan cheese**

salt and **pepper**

2 tablespoons **olive oil**

1 large **onion**, finely chopped

1 **butternut squash**, about 875 g (1¾ lb), peeled, deseeded and cut into cubes

1 **sweet potato**, about 300 g (10 oz), peeled and cut into cubes

3.5 cm (1½ inch) piece of fresh **root ginger**, peeled and finely chopped

2 **garlic cloves**, chopped (optional)

900 ml (1½ pints) **Vegetable Stock** (see page 19)

450 ml (¾ pint) semi-skimmed **milk**

salt and **pepper**

CROÛTONS:

1 **poppy seed bagel**, cut into cubes

2 tablespoons **olive oil**

20

PREP

50

COOK

6

SERVES

hearty

Squash, sweet potato and ginger soup

Velvety smooth, with a wonderful vibrant colour, this soup makes an ideal quick lunch and is smart enough to serve to friends, if dressed up with a swirl of cream.

1 Heat the oil in a large, heavy-based saucepan, add the onion and cook over a moderate heat for about 5 minutes or until softened. Add the butternut squash, sweet potato, ginger and garlic (if using) and cook, stirring, for 3 minutes.

2 Pour in the stock, season to taste with salt and pepper and bring to the boil. Reduce the heat, cover and simmer for 30 minutes or until reduced and thickened. In a blender or food processor, blend the soup in batches until smooth, then return it to the pan. Stir in the milk and set aside until ready to reheat.

3 Just before serving, put the bagel cubes into a plastic bag with the oil, toss together and transfer to a baking sheet. Bake in a pre-heated oven, 200°C (400°F), Gas Mark 6, for 10 minutes or until golden. Reheat the soup gently, then ladle into warm bowls and serve immediately sprinkled with the croûtons.

Butternut squash and tofu soup

It's unusual in traditional Chinese cooking to find the blended soups so often seen in other parts of the world. This recipe is so creamy that you might think it contains milk or cream. You can use pumpkin instead of the butternut squash if you prefer.

1 Put the onion in a large, heavy-based saucepan, cover and leave to sweat over a low heat for 10 minutes.

2 Add the carrots, butternut squash, ginger and stock and bring to the boil.

3 Reduce the heat and simmer gently for 25–30 minutes until all the vegetables are tender. Add the tofu, stir well and return the soup to the boil.

4 In a blender or food processor, blend the soup until smooth and creamy. Ladle into warm soup bowls and serve immediately.

15

PREP

45

COOK

4

SERVES

easy

1 large **onion**, roughly chopped

150 g (5 oz) **carrots**, cut into large cubes

1 butternut squash, 625–750 g (1¼–1½ lb), cut into large cubes

1 slice of fresh **root ginger**

600 ml (1 pint) **Vegetable Stock** (see page 19)

250 g (8 oz) silken **tofu**, roughly chopped

500 g (1 lb) **chestnuts**

1 tablespoon **olive oil**

125 g (4 oz) rindless **smoked bacon**, diced

1 large **onion**, chopped

2 **celery sticks**, chopped

2 **carrots**, chopped

1 **bouquet garni**

1.2 litres (2 pints) **Chicken Stock** (see page 17)

salt and **pepper**

TO GARNISH:

grilled **bacon**, crumbled

chopped **parsley**

40

PREP

75

COOK

8

SERVES

party

Cream of chestnut soup

This simple recipe relies on fresh, quality ingredients. The bacon and chestnuts are given plenty of time to cook, during which they combine to produce a rounded flavour that's unusual but delicious.

1 Cut a slash in the pointed end of each chestnut. Place in a saucepan, cover with cold water and bring to the boil, then reduce the heat and simmer for 2 minutes. Remove from the heat. Using a slotted spoon, lift out one chestnut at a time and remove and discard the outer and inner skins. If the skins are hard to peel, return the pan to the boil and repeat.

2 Heat the oil in a large, heavy-based saucepan, add the diced bacon and onion and cook over a moderate heat for 2 minutes without browning. Add the celery, carrots and bouquet garni and stir well. Add the stock and salt and pepper to taste. Add the peeled chestnuts and bring to the boil. Reduce the heat, cover and simmer for 1 hour or until the chestnuts are tender. Remove and discard the bouquet garni and leave to cool slightly

3 In a blender or food processor, blend the soup in batches until smooth, returning to the pan. Reheat gently. Ladle into warm soup bowls, garnish with crumbled grilled bacon and chopped parsley and serve immediately.

Herbed tomato and lemon broth

Plum tomatoes usually have a more intense, tomatoey flavour than other varieties. They work well with spicy ingredients, and the Tabasco sauce gives the soup a lively twist that will be tempered slightly by the fresh oregano and parsley.

1 Drain the tomatoes, reserving half of the juice. Melt the butter in a large, heavy-based saucepan, add the tomatoes and cook over a moderate heat, stirring and breaking them up with a wooden spoon, for 5 minutes.

2 Add the reserved tomato juice, stock, lemon juice and rind and plenty of pepper. Stir in the sugar, Tabasco or hot pepper sauce and Worcestershire sauce. Bring to the boil. Reduce the heat and simmer for 15 minutes.

3 Stir in the oregano and parsley and simmer the soup for a further 5 minutes.

4 In a blender or food processor, blend the soup until smooth. Reheat briefly in a clean saucepan. Ladle into warm soup bowls, garnish each portion with a lemon slice and serve immediately.

5 PREP

30 COOK

4 SERVES

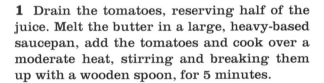

fresh

400 g (13 oz) can **plum tomatoes**

25 g (1 oz) **butter**

600 ml (1 pint) **Vegetable Stock** (see page 19)

2 tablespoons **lemon juice**

1 teaspoon grated **lemon rind**

½ teaspoon **caster sugar**

4 drops of **Tabasco sauce** or **hot pepper sauce** (or to taste)

2 teaspoons **Worcestershire sauce**

1 tablespoon chopped **oregano**

1 tablespoon chopped **parsley**

pepper

4 thin **lemon** slices, to garnish

1 kg (2 lb) vine-ripened **tomatoes**, roughly chopped

2 **garlic cloves**, crushed

300 ml (½ pint) **Vegetable Stock** (see page 19)

2 tablespoons extra virgin **olive oil**

1 teaspoon **caster sugar**

100 g (3½ oz) **ground almonds**, toasted

salt and **pepper**

BASIL OIL:

150 ml (¼ pint) extra virgin **olive oil**

15 g (½ oz) **basil leaves**

15

PREP

20

COOK

4

SERVES

easy

Fresh tomato and almond soup

The addition of ground almonds not only flavours this delicious soup but helps to thicken it as well. Make it during the summer months when tomatoes are at their juiciest and best. To toast the almonds, dry-fry them in a frying pan over a medium heat, stirring constantly until they are golden brown.

1 Put the tomatoes in a large, heavy-based saucepan with the garlic, stock, oil and sugar. Season to taste with salt and pepper. Bring to the boil, then reduce the heat and simmer gently for 15 minutes.

2 Meanwhile, make the basil oil. In a blender or food processor, blend the oil and basil leaves with a pinch of salt until really smooth. Set aside.

3 Stir the ground almonds into the soup, heat through and then serve in warm soup bowls, drizzled with the basil oil.

Tomato and bread soup

This classic Italian soup is often served at room temperature, but this is a hot version, which brings together the great combination of tomato and basil. If you prefer, you can leave the soup to cool to room temperature before serving.

1 Put the tomatoes in a large, heavy-based saucepan with the stock, 2 tablespoons of the oil, the garlic, sugar and basil and slowly bring to the boil. Reduce the heat, cover and simmer gently for 30 minutes.

2 Crumble the bread into the soup and stir over a low heat until thickened. Stir in the vinegar and the remaining oil and season to taste with salt and pepper. Spoon into warm soup bowls and stir a spoonful of pesto into each bowl before serving, if liked.

15
PREP

40
COOK

4
SERVES

classic

1 kg (2 lb) vine-ripened **tomatoes**, skinned, deseeded and chopped

300 ml (½ pint) **Vegetable Stock** (see page 19)

6 tablespoons extra virgin **olive oil**

2 **garlic cloves**, crushed

1 teaspoon **caster sugar**

2 tablespoons chopped **basil**

100 g (3½ oz) day-old **bread**, without crusts

1 tablespoon **balsamic vinegar**

salt and **pepper**

pesto, to serve (optional)

3 tablespoons **olive oil**

1 **onion**, chopped

1 **carrot**, chopped

2 **celery sticks**, sliced

1 **garlic clove**, chopped

750 g (1½ lb) peeled and chopped **aubergine**

1.2 litres (2 pints) **Vegetable Stock** (see page 19)

2 tablespoons roughly chopped **basil**

2 tablespoons grated **Parmesan cheese**

1 tablespoon **medium dry sherry**

125 ml (4 fl oz) **double cream**

salt and **pepper**

25

PREP

75

COOK

4

SERVES

stylish

Aubergine soup

Another name for this unique vegetable is eggplant, because these fruiting vegetables grow to the size and shape of eggs in their native East Indies. They have a distinctive, slightly smoky flavour.

1 Heat the oil in a large, heavy-based saucepan and add the onion, carrot, celery, garlic and aubergine. Cover tightly and cook over a low heat, stirring frequently, for 15–18 minutes or until softened.

2 Add the stock and bring to the boil. Reduce the heat, cover and simmer for 1 hour or until the vegetables are very tender. Add the basil and leave to cool slightly.

3 In a blender or food processor, blend the soup in batches until smooth, then transfer it to a clean saucepan.

4 Stir in the Parmesan, sherry and cream. Reheat gently without boiling and season to taste with salt and pepper. Ladle into warm soup bowls and serve immediately.

Bright red pepper soup

A vibrant and warming soup, this can be served at any meal and it tastes just as good warm or cold.

15

PREP

40

COOK

4

SERVES

simple

2 tablespoons **olive oil**

2 **onions**, finely chopped

1 **garlic clove**, crushed (optional)

3 **red peppers**, cored, deseeded and roughly chopped

2 **courgettes**, roughly chopped

900 ml (1½ pints) **Vegetable Stock** (see page 19) or **water**

salt and **pepper**

TO SERVE:

natural yogurt or **double cream**

snipped **chives**

1 Heat the oil in a large, heavy-based saucepan, add the onions and cook over a moderate heat for about 5 minutes or until softened. Add the garlic (if using) and cook, stirring, for 1 minute.

2 Add all the red peppers and half of the courgettes to the pan and cook for 5–8 minutes or until softened and browned.

3 Add the stock, season to taste with salt and pepper and bring to the boil. Reduce the heat, cover and simmer gently for 20 minutes or until the vegetables are tender.

4 In a blender or food processor, blend the soup in batches until smooth, then transfer it to a clean saucepan. Check and adjust the seasoning if necessary. Reheat the soup gently and serve topped with the remaining chopped courgette, yogurt or a swirl of cream and snipped chives.

6 large **red peppers**

3 tablespoons **olive oil**

4 **leeks**, white and pale green parts only, thinly sliced

750 ml (1¼ pints) **Vegetable Stock** (see page 19)

75 ml (3 fl oz) **mascarpone cheese**

75 ml (3 fl oz) **milk**

2 teaspoons **black peppercorns**, finely ground

salt and **pepper**

toasted country **bread**, to serve

20[*]

PREP

60

COOK

4

SERVES

spicy

Red pepper soup with pepper cream

The smoky, sweet flavour of roasted peppers is given a pungent kick by the addition of black pepper. Black pepper is fundamental to much Italian cooking, especially in the north.

1 Put the red peppers in a large roasting tin and roast in a preheated oven, 240°C (475°F), Gas Mark 9, for 20–30 minutes, turning once, until beginning to char. Remove from the oven and transfer to a plastic bag. Close tightly and leave to steam for 10 minutes.

2 Remove the peppers from the bag and peel off the skins. Pull out the stalks – the seeds should come with them. Halve, scrape out any remaining seeds and roughly chop the flesh.

3 Heat the oil in a large, heavy-based saucepan, add the leeks and cook over a low heat for 10 minutes. Add the peppers, stock and a little salt and pepper. Bring to the boil. Reduce the heat and simmer for 20 minutes. Meanwhile, in a bowl, beat the mascarpone with the milk and ground peppercorns. Season to taste with salt, cover and chill.

4 In a blender or food processor, blend the soup in batches until smooth, then transfer it to a clean saucepan. Reheat gently. Serve in warm soup bowls with dollops of the pepper cream and slices of toasted country bread.

* Plus 10 minutes steaming

Roasted pepper and tomato soup

To remove the pepper skins quickly, hold them under cold running water and simply rub the charred skins away. This also makes them cool enough to handle easily.

10*

PREP

45

COOK

4

SERVES

tasty

4 **red peppers**, halved, cored and deseeded

500 g (1 lb) **tomatoes**, halved

1 teaspoon **olive oil**

1 **onion**, chopped

1 **carrot**, chopped

600 ml (1 pint) **Vegetable Stock** (see page 19)

2 tablespoons light **crème fraîche**

handful of **basil**, torn into pieces

pepper

1 Arrange the red peppers skin side up and the tomatoes skin side down on a baking sheet and cook under a preheated high grill for 8–10 minutes until the skins of the peppers are charred. Remove from the grill and transfer to a plastic bag. Close tightly and leave to steam for 10 minutes. Leave the tomatoes to cool.

2 Remove the peppers from the bag and peel off the skins. Slice the flesh. Peel off the skins of the tomatoes.

3 Heat the oil in a large, heavy-based saucepan, add the onion and carrot and cook over a moderate heat for 5 minutes. Add the stock, peppers and tomatoes and bring to the boil, then reduce the heat and simmer for 25 minutes until the carrot is tender.

4 In a blender or food processor, blend the soup in batches until smooth, then put it into a clean saucepan. Reheat gently. Stir through the crème fraîche and basil. Season well with pepper and serve in warm soup bowls.

* Plus 10 minutes steaming

3 **yellow peppers**, halved, cored and deseeded

75 g (3 oz) **butter**

1 small **onion**, chopped

1.2 litres (2 pints) **Vegetable Stock** (see page 19)

1 teaspoon mild **curry powder**

¼ teaspoon **ground turmeric**

1 tablespoon chopped fresh **coriander**

300 g (10 oz) **potatoes**, chopped

salt

20
PREP

55
COOK

4
SERVES

hearty

Yellow pepper soup

Slightly sweet, yellow peppers are milder in flavour than green ones. This quick and easy soup is an excellent choice for lunch.

1 Chop half of 1 yellow pepper finely and put in a small saucepan. Chop the remaining peppers roughly.

2 Melt 50 g (2 oz) of the butter in a large, heavy-based saucepan, add the onion and roughly chopped peppers and cook over a moderate heat for 5 minutes. Stir in the stock, curry powder, turmeric and coriander, then add the potatoes. Bring to the boil. Reduce the heat, partially cover and simmer for 40–45 minutes or until the vegetables are tender.

3 Meanwhile, melt the remaining butter with the finely chopped pepper in the small pan. Cook over a low heat until the pepper is very tender. Set aside for the garnish.

4 In a blender or food processor, blend the soup in batches until smooth, then transfer it to a clean saucepan. Reheat gently. Serve in warm soup bowls, garnishing each portion with a little of the finely chopped pepper.

Fennel and lemon soup

20
PREP

40
COOK

4
SERVES

posh

Fennel, lemon and black olives are a perfect combination of flavours. To give this soup a summery flavour, use fat salad onions, like giant spring onions, which you sometimes see in bunches in early summer. Use Greek-style, crinkled black olives with their full ripe fruity flavour for the gremolata.

1 Heat the oil in a large, heavy-based saucepan, add the onions and cook over a moderate heat for 5 minutes or until softened. Add the sliced fennel, potato and lemon rind and cook for 5 minutes or until the fennel begins to soften.

2 Add the stock and bring to the boil. Reduce the heat, cover and simmer for 25 minutes or until all the vegetables are tender.

3 Meanwhile, make the gremolata. Mix the garlic, lemon rind, fennel fronds and parsley. Stir in the olives, cover and chill.

4 In a blender or food processor, blend the soup in batches until smooth. Press through a sieve to remove any remaining strings of fennel and transfer to a clean saucepan. Reheat gently. The soup should not be too thick, so add more stock if necessary. Taste and season well with salt and pepper and plenty of lemon juice. Ladle into warm soup bowls and sprinkle each serving with a portion of the gremolata, which should be stirred in before eating.

75 ml (3 fl oz) extra virgin **olive oil**

3 **salad onions**, chopped

250 g (8 oz) **fennel**, trimmed and thinly sliced, any fronds reserved and finely chopped for the gremolata

1 **potato**, diced

finely grated rind and juice of 1 **lemon**

750 ml (1¼ pints) **Vegetable Stock** (see page 19)

salt and **pepper**

BLACK OLIVE GREMOLATA:

1 small **garlic clove**, finely chopped

finely grated rind of 1 **lemon**

4 tablespoons chopped **parsley**

16 Greek-style **black olives**, pitted and chopped

900 ml (1½ pints) **Vegetable Stock** (see page 19)

2 **fennel bulbs**, trimmed and chopped

1 **onion**, chopped

1 **courgette**, chopped

1 **carrot**, chopped

2 **garlic cloves**, thinly sliced

400 g (13 oz) can **tomatoes**

2 x 400 g (13 oz) cans **butter beans**, rinsed and drained

2 tablespoons chopped **sage**

pepper

15

PREP

40

COOK

4

SERVES

easy

Fennel and white bean soup

If you are using fresh tomatoes and have enough time, it's worth removing the skins. To do this, cut a small cross at the top of each tomato and put them in a heatproof bowl of boiling water for a couple of minutes. The skins should peel off easily.

1 Put 300 ml (½ pint) of the stock in a large, heavy-based saucepan and add the fennel, onion, courgette, carrot and garlic. Cover and bring to the boil. Boil for 5 minutes. Uncover, reduce the heat and simmer gently for 20 minutes or until all the vegetables are tender.

2 Stir in the tomatoes, beans and sage. Season to taste with pepper and pour in the remaining stock. Simmer for 5 minutes, then leave the soup to cool slightly.

3 In a blender or food processor, blend 300 ml (½ pint) of the soup until smooth. Return to the pan and reheat gently. Serve the soup immediately in warm soup bowls.

Parsnip and fennel soup

15

PREP

40

COOK

4

SERVES

filling

These two flavoursome vegetables make the ideal partnership in this deliciously creamy soup. It makes quite a filling meal, but you should serve it with plenty of warmed bread for dunking.

1 Melt the butter in a large, heavy-based saucepan, add the parsnips, fennel and onion and cook over a moderate heat, stirring frequently, for about 15 minutes until all the vegetables are tender.

2 In a small bowl, blend the cornflour with 150 ml (¼ pint) of the hot stock until thick and smooth. Fold into the vegetables, then pour in the remaining hot stock, stirring the mixture constantly.

3 Bring to the boil, stirring, then reduce the heat, partially cover and simmer, stirring frequently, for 20 minutes. Season to taste with salt and pepper, stir in the cream and heat through gently without boiling. Serve immediately in warm soup bowls.

50 g (2 oz) **butter**

500 g (1 lb) **parsnips**, scrubbed and cut into 5 mm (¼ inch) dice

500 g (1 lb) **fennel bulb**, trimmed and diced

1 **onion**, chopped

3 tablespoons **cornflour**

1.2 litres (2 pints) hot **Vegetable Stock** (see page 19)

150 ml (¼ pint) **double cream**

salt and **pepper**

25 g (1 oz) **butter**

50 g (2 oz) fresh **root ginger**, peeled and thinly sliced

1 bunch of **spring onions**

500 g (1 lb) **parsnips**, sliced

1 litre (1¾ pints) **Vegetable Stock** (see page 19)

salt and **pepper**

crème fraîche, to serve

10

PREP

20

COOK

4

SERVES

thick

Fresh ginger and parsnip soup

This simple soup has Asian influences. Crème fraîche is a lovely garnish for all manner of soups, as it begins to sink into the hot liquid and adds a cool, creamy taste.

1 Melt the butter in a large, heavy-based saucepan, add the ginger and cook over a moderate heat, stirring, for 1 minute. Reserve 1 spring onion, roughly chop the remainder and add to the pan with the parsnips. Cook, stirring, for 2 minutes.

2 Add the stock and bring to the boil, then reduce the heat, cover and simmer gently for 15 minutes or until the parsnips are tender. Meanwhile, shred the reserved spring onion lengthways into fine ribbons.

3 In a blender or food processor, blend the soup in batches until smooth, then return it to the pan. Season to taste with salt and pepper and reheat gently for 1 minute.

4 Ladle into warm soup bowls and serve topped with a spoonful of crème fraîche and scattered with the spring onion ribbons.

Curried parsnip soup

Parsnips and spices are blended to create a warming soup with an Indian flavour. If you prefer a milder flavour, use less curry powder or choose a milder version.

15

PREP

45

COOK

6

SERVES

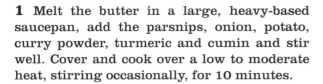

spicy

125 g (4 oz) **butter**

1.5 kg (3 lb) **parsnips**, scrubbed and roughly chopped

1 **onion**, chopped

1 **potato**, chopped

1 tablespoon medium hot **curry powder**

1 teaspoon **ground turmeric**

½ teaspoon **ground cumin**

1.8 litres (3 pints) **Vegetable Stock** (see page 19)

150 ml (¼ pint) **double cream**

salt and **pepper**

snipped **chives** or finely chopped **parsley**, to garnish

1 Melt the butter in a large, heavy-based saucepan, add the parsnips, onion, potato, curry powder, turmeric and cumin and stir well. Cover and cook over a low to moderate heat, stirring occasionally, for 10 minutes.

2 Add the stock and bring to the boil. Reduce the heat, cover and simmer for 30 minutes. Add a little water if the soup is too thick.

3 In a blender or food processor, blend the soup in batches, then transfer it to a clean saucepan. Reheat gently and stir in the cream. Serve the soup immediately in warm soup bowls, garnishing each portion with a sprinkling of chives or parsley.

2 tablespoons **olive oil**

1 **onion**, finely chopped

1 **baking potato**, about 275 g (9 oz), diced

1 **garlic clove**, chopped

200 g (7 oz) can **tomatoes**

900 ml (1½ pints) **Vegetable Stock** (see page 19)

175 g (6 oz) **broccoli**, cut into tiny florets and stalks sliced

125 g (4 oz) frozen **peas**

2 teaspoons **pesto**, plus extra to garnish

salt and **pepper**

TO GARNISH:

grated **Parmesan cheese**

handful of **basil** leaves

15

PREP

30

COOK

4

SERVES

herby

Quick pesto, pea and broccoli soup

This hearty vegetable soup is full of Italian flavour. If you prefer, use four fresh, skinned and chopped tomatoes instead of the canned tomatoes. To make the soup more substantial, add a small can of cannellini or white kidney beans, or small soup pasta.

1 Heat the oil in a large, heavy-based saucepan, add the onion and cook over a moderate heat for 5–6 minutes or until lightly browned. Add the potato and garlic and cook, stirring frequently, for 5 minutes or until the potato is softened.

2 Add the tomatoes and stock, season to taste with salt and pepper and bring to the boil. Reduce the heat, cover and simmer for 10 minutes or until reduced and thickened. Add the broccoli, peas and pesto and simmer for a further 3–4 minutes or until the broccoli is just tender.

3 Ladle the soup into warm soup bowls. Serve garnished with a little extra pesto, grated Parmesan and basil leaves.

Creamy broccoli and almond soup

Keep a watchful eye on the clock while you're making this soup because overcooking will result in a duller green soup, not the pretty, speckled green effect you're aiming at. If you prefer, use semi-skimmed milk and low-fat cream cheese for a lighter result.

1 Heat the butter and oil in a large, heavy-based saucepan, add the onion and potato and cook over a moderate heat for 5 minutes or until softened but not browned.

2 Cut the broccoli into florets and slice the stalks. Add to the pan together with the stock and bring to the boil. Reduce the heat, cover and simmer for 8 minutes or until all the vegetables are just tender.

3 In a blender or food processor, blend the soup with the almonds, milk and cream cheese in batches until smooth, then return it to the pan. Season to taste with salt and pepper and nutmeg. Reheat gently without boiling. Ladle the soup into warm soup bowls. Serve garnished with the toasted flaked almonds and paprika.

20
PREP

20
COOK

4
SERVES

rich

15 g (½ oz) **butter**

1 tablespoon **olive oil**

1 **onion**, roughly chopped

150 g (5 oz) **potato**, finely diced

300 g (10 oz) **broccoli**

450 ml (¾ pint) **Vegetable Stock** (see page 19)

3 tablespoons **flaked almonds**

450 ml (¾ pint) **milk**

100 g (3½ oz) **cream cheese**

grated nutmeg, to taste

salt and **pepper**

TO GARNISH:

2 tablespoons **flaked almonds**, toasted

a little **paprika**

1 kg (2 lb) **green broccoli**

50 g (2 oz) **butter**

1 **onion**, chopped

1 large **potato**, quartered

1 tablespoon medium hot **curry powder**

1.5 litres (2½ pints) **Vegetable Stock** (see page 19)

150 ml (¼ pint) **single cream**

salt and **pepper**

15

PREP

35

COOK

6

SERVES

thick

Curried cream of broccoli soup

There are several types of broccoli available, including purple- and white-flowered forms. In this soup, green broccoli, or calabrese, is used. Try not to overcook it, which will spoil the flavour.

1 Cut off the broccoli stalks, peel and slice them into 2.5 cm (1 inch) pieces. Break the florets into very small pieces and reserve.

2 Melt the butter in a large, heavy-based saucepan and add the onion and broccoli stalks. Cover and cook over a moderate heat, stirring frequently, for 5 minutes.

3 Add the reserved florets, potato, curry powder and stock. Bring to the boil, partially cover and cook for 5 minutes. Using a slotted spoon, remove 6 florets for the garnish and reserve. Season to taste with salt and pepper. Cook over a moderate heat for a further 20 minutes or until all the vegetables are tender.

4 In a blender or food processor, blend the soup in batches until smooth, then transfer it to a clean saucepan. Add the cream and reheat gently without boiling. Serve the soup in warm bowls, garnishing each one with some of the reserved florets.

Broccoli and cheese soup

15

PREP

35

COOK

This is a variation of Curried Cream of Broccoli Soup (opposite). The cream and cheese make this quite a rich, thick soup, so if you're serving it as a starter, you will need only a small amount per person.

6

SERVES

thick

1 Cut off the broccoli stalks, peel and slice them into 2.5 cm (1 inch) pieces. Break the florets into very small pieces and reserve.

2 Melt the butter in a large, heavy-based saucepan and add the onion and broccoli stalks. Cover and cook over a moderate heat, stirring frequently, for 5 minutes.

3 Add the reserved florets, potato, curry powder and stock. Bring to the boil, partially cover and cook for 5 minutes. Using a slotted spoon, remove 6 florets for the garnish and reserve. Season to taste with salt and pepper. Cook over a moderate heat for 20 minutes or until all the vegetables are tender.

4 In a blender or food processor, blend the soup in batches until smooth, then transfer it to a clean saucepan. Add the cream, lemon juice, Worcestershire sauce and Tabasco sauce. Simmer gently for 3–5 minutes without boiling. Stir in the grated cheese, then serve immediately in warm soup bowls.

1 kg (2 lb) **green broccoli**

50 g (2 oz) **butter**

1 **onion**, chopped

1 large **potato**, quartered

1.5 litres (2½ pints) **Vegetable Stock** (see page 19)

125 ml (4 fl oz) **single cream**

1 tablespoon **lemon juice**

1 teaspoon **Worcestershire sauce**

few drops of **Tabasco sauce** (or to taste)

125 g (4 oz) mature **Cheddar cheese**, grated

salt and **pepper**

50 g (2 oz) **butter**

2 tablespoons **olive oil**

1 **onion**, diced

1 **garlic clove**, chopped

2 **potatoes**, chopped

250 g (8 oz) **broccoli**, chopped

300 g (10 oz) **spinach**, chopped

900 ml (1½ pints) **Vegetable Stock** (see page 19)

125 g (4 oz) **Gorgonzola cheese**, crumbled into small pieces

2 tablespoons **lemon juice**

½ teaspoon **grated nutmeg**

salt and **pepper**

75 g (3 oz) toasted **pine nuts**, to garnish

warm crusty **bread**, to serve

10

PREP

20

COOK

4

SERVES

simple

Spinach and broccoli soup

Spinach and blue cheese are a match made in heaven! The cheese will start to melt into the liquid and can be mopped up with warm crusty bread.

1 Melt the butter with the oil in a large, heavy-based saucepan, add the onion and garlic and cook over a moderate heat for about 3 minutes.

2 Add the potatoes, broccoli, spinach and stock and bring to the boil. Reduce the heat and simmer for 15 minutes.

3 The soup can be blended at this stage in a blender or food processor or left with chunky pieces. Add the Gorgonzola with the lemon juice, nutmeg and salt and pepper to taste. Garnish with the toasted pine nuts and serve immediately with warm crusty bread.

Spinach and mushroom soup

This is a great way to enjoy mushrooms. The soup is left unblended so that they retain their texture. Make sure you use baby spinach, because the leaves are smaller and more delicate, making them better suited to this particular recipe.

1 Melt the butter with the oil in a large, heavy-based saucepan, add the onion and cook over a moderate heat for 5 minutes. Add the mushrooms and garlic and cook, stirring, for 3 minutes.

2 Stir in the ginger and stock. Bring to the boil, then reduce the heat, cover and simmer gently for 10 minutes.

3 Add the spinach and nutmeg and simmer gently for 2 minutes. Season to taste with salt and pepper and serve immediately in warm soup bowls, scattered with croûtons.

5
PREP

20
COOK

4
SERVES

light

50 g (2 oz) **butter**

1 tablespoon **groundnut oil** or **vegetable oil**

1 **onion**, finely chopped

150 g (5 oz) **shiitake mushrooms**

175 g (6 oz) **chestnut mushrooms** or **cup mushrooms**

2 **garlic cloves**, crushed

5 cm (2 inch) piece of fresh **root ginger**, peeled and grated

1 litre (1¾ pints) **Vegetable Stock** (see page 19)

225 g (7½ oz) **baby spinach**

plenty of **grated nutmeg**

salt and **pepper**

croûtons, to serve

2 tablespoons extra virgin **olive oil**, plus extra to serve

1 **onion**, finely chopped

2 **garlic cloves**, finely chopped

300 g (10 oz) **baby spinach**, roughly shredded

900 ml (1½ pints) **Vegetable Stock** (see page 19)

175 g (6 oz) **arborio rice**

4 **eggs**

salt and **pepper**

grated **Parmesan cheese**, to serve (optional)

PREP

COOK

4

SERVES

hearty

Spinach and rice soup

This delicious, hearty soup contains poached eggs, making it a nutritious meal in itself. Poaching the eggs in the soup is also a great way to save time – and it saves on the washing up, too!

1 Heat the oil in a large, heavy-based saucepan, add the onion and garlic and cook over a moderate heat for 5 minutes or until softened. Add the spinach and cook, stirring, until wilted.

2 Add the stock and rice and season to taste with salt and pepper. Bring to the boil, then reduce the heat, cover and simmer gently for 15 minutes or until the rice is tender.

3 Carefully break the eggs into the soup so that they sit on the surface. Cover and cook gently for 5–6 minutes or until the eggs are poached. Serve the soup in warm soup bowls, drizzled with a little extra olive oil and some grated Parmesan, if liked.

Spinach and potato soup

Although frozen leaf spinach can be used for this recipe, the full-flavoured taste of fresh spinach cannot be equalled.

10
PREP

20
COOK

4
SERVES

rich

1 Melt the butter in a large, heavy-based saucepan, add the onion and cook over a moderate heat for 5 minutes or until softened but not browned. Add the spinach and cook, stirring, until wilted.

2 Add the stock, potatoes, lemon juice and nutmeg and season to taste with salt and pepper. Bring to the boil, then reduce the heat, partially cover and simmer for 10–12 minutes or until the potatoes are tender.

3 In a blender or food processor, blend the soup in batches until smooth, then transfer it to a clean saucepan. Add the cream and reheat gently without boiling. Serve the soup in warm bowls, garnished with a sprinkling of ground almonds, if liked.

50 g (2 oz) **butter**

1 **onion**, finely chopped

500 g (1 lb) fresh or frozen **spinach**

1.2 litres (2 pints) **Vegetable Stock** (see page 19)

250 g (8 oz) **potatoes**, thinly sliced

1 teaspoon **lemon juice**

pinch of **grated nutmeg**

150 ml (¼ pint) **double cream**

salt and **white pepper**

ground almonds, to garnish (optional)

1 tablespoon **olive oil**

1 small **red onion**, finely chopped

1 **garlic clove**, finely chopped

1 **carrot**, diced

2 **celery sticks**, chopped

400 g (13 oz) can chopped **tomatoes**

1 tablespoon **sun-dried tomato paste**

600 ml (1 pint) **Vegetable Stock** (see page 19)

750 g (1½ lb) can **mixed beans**, drained and rinsed

3 tablespoons chopped **flat leaf parsley**

salt and **pepper**

pesto, to serve

10
PREP

40
COOK

4
SERVES

filling

Tuscan bean soup

This rustic soup is based on the classic Italian version and uses the common combination of tomatoes, onion and garlic as a base. Mixed beans provide the bulk for the soup, and you can either use a can of mixed beans or the equivalent weight of your own choosing.

1 Heat the oil in a large, heavy-based saucepan, add the onion and cook over a moderate heat for about 5 minutes or until softened. Stir in the garlic, carrot and celery and cook for 5 minutes.

2 Add the tomatoes, tomato paste and stock. Season to taste with salt and pepper. Bring to the boil, then reduce the heat and simmer, stirring occasionally, for 20–30 minutes or until the vegetables are tender.

3 In a blender or food processor, blend half of the soup until smooth. Return to the pan. Add the beans to the soup and simmer for a further 10 minutes until heated through. Stir in the parsley, then serve immediately in warm soup bowls, garnished with a spoonful of pesto.

Chilli bean soup

This is a soup version of vegetarian chilli, and it is packed full of lovely warming spices. The tortilla chip and melted cheese topping makes an unusual garnish and should help turn this into a family favourite.

1 Heat the oil in a large, heavy-based saucepan, add the onion, garlic, chilli powder, coriander and cumin and cook over a moderate heat, stirring frequently, for about 5 minutes until the onion has softened. Add the beans, tomatoes and stock and season to taste with salt and pepper.

2 Bring to the boil, then reduce the heat, cover and simmer for 15 minutes.

3 In a blender or food processor, blend the soup in batches until fairly smooth. Pour into ovenproof soup bowls.

4 Arrange the tortilla chips on top of the soup, scatter over the grated cheese and cook under a preheated high grill for 1–2 minutes or until the cheese has melted. Serve the soup immediately with soured cream.

10
PREP

25
COOK

3

SERVES

feast

2 tablespoons **olive oil**

1 **onion**, chopped

1 **garlic clove**, crushed

1 teaspoon hot **chilli powder**

1 teaspoon **ground coriander**

½ teaspoon **ground cumin**

400 g (13 oz) can **red kidney beans**, rinsed and drained

400 g (13 oz) can chopped **tomatoes**

600 ml (1 pint) **Vegetable Stock** (see page 19)

12 **tortilla chips**

50 g (2 oz) **Cheddar cheese**, grated

salt and **pepper**

soured cream, to serve

3 tablespoons **olive oil**

1 **onion**, finely chopped

2 **celery sticks**, thinly sliced

2 **garlic cloves**, thinly sliced

2 x 425 g (14 oz) cans **butter beans**, rinsed and drained

4 tablespoons **sun-dried tomato paste**

900 ml (1½ pints) **Vegetable Stock** (see page 19)

1 tablespoon chopped **rosemary** or **thyme**

salt and **pepper**

Parmesan cheese shavings, to serve

5

PREP

20

COOK

4

SERVES

easy

Butter bean and sun-dried tomato soup

Although it takes only a few minutes to make, this chunky soup distinctly resembles a robust Italian minestrone. It will make a worthy main course served with bread and plenty of Parmesan.

1 Heat the oil in a large, heavy-based saucepan, add the onion and cook over a moderate heat for about 5 minutes until softened. Add the celery and garlic and cook, stirring, for 2 minutes.

2 Add the beans, tomato paste, stock and rosemary or thyme. Season to taste with salt and pepper and bring to the boil. Reduce the heat, cover and simmer gently for 15 minutes. Serve in warm soup bowls sprinkled with Parmesan shavings.

Smooth red bean soup

The red kidney beans, chilli and tomatoes give this recipe a real Mexican flavour. If you don't have much time but would still like to make the soup, you could use canned beans instead of dried.

1 Drain the beans in a colander, rinse under cold running water and drain again. Put in a saucepan with cold water to cover. Bring to the boil. Boil rapidly for 10 minutes, skimming off the scum that rises to the surface. Drain.

2 Heat the oil in a large, heavy-based saucepan, add the onion, garlic, red pepper and carrot and cook over a moderate heat for 5 minutes. Add all the spices and herbs, stock, measured water, beans, tomato purée and tomatoes and stir well to break up the tomatoes. Bring to the boil, then reduce the heat, partially cover and simmer for 1¼ hours, skimming off any scum that rises to the surface. Remove and discard the bay leaf.

3 In a blender or food processor, blend the soup until smooth, then strain through a sieve into a clean saucepan. Add salt to taste. Add a little more water if the soup is too thick. Reheat gently without boiling. Serve in warm soup bowls, garnishing each portion with a swirl of soured cream.

15*
PREP

100
COOK

6
SERVES

thick

250 g (8 oz) dried red **kidney beans**, soaked overnight in cold water

3 tablespoons **olive oil**

1 **onion**, chopped

2 **garlic cloves**, chopped

1 **red pepper**, cored, deseeded and chopped

1 **carrot**, chopped

¼ teaspoon **cayenne pepper**

1 teaspoon mild **chilli powder**

¼ teaspoon **dried thyme**

1 **bay leaf**

1 small sprig of **rosemary**

600 ml (1 pint) **Vegetable Stock** (see page 19)

1.2 litres (2 pints) **water**

2 tablespoons **tomato purée**

400 g (13 oz) can peeled **plum tomatoes**

salt

150 ml (¼ pint) **soured cream**, to garnish

* Plus overnight soaking

3 tablespoons **olive oil**

2 **onions**, sliced

2 **bay leaves**

175 g (6 oz) **green lentils**, washed and drained

1 litre (1¾ pints) **Vegetable Stock** (see page 19)

½ teaspoon **ground turmeric**

small handful of fresh **coriander**, roughly chopped

salt and **pepper**

SPICED BUTTER:

50 g (2 oz) lightly salted **butter**, softened

1 large **garlic clove**, crushed

1 teaspoon **paprika**

1 teaspoon **cumin seeds**

1 **red chilli**, deseeded and thinly sliced

10

PREP

25

COOK

4

SERVES

spicy

Green lentil soup with spiced butter

Serve the spicy butter separately for stirring into the soup, so that each person can 'gee up' their own portion according to personal taste.

1 Heat the oil in a large, heavy-based saucepan, add the onions and cook over a moderate heat for 3 minutes. Add the bay leaves, lentils, stock and turmeric. Bring to the boil, then reduce the heat, cover and simmer for 20 minutes or until the lentils are tender and turning mushy.

2 Meanwhile, make the spiced butter. In a bowl, beat the butter with the remaining ingredients. Transfer to a small serving dish.

3 Stir the coriander into the soup, season to taste with salt and pepper and serve with the spiced butter in a separate bowl at the table for stirring into the soup.

Lentil and pea soup with crème fraîche

Be sure to use homemade vegetable stock in this recipe. The extra effort is more than made up for by the extra depth of flavour, and if you make a particularly large batch, you can always freeze it.

1 Heat the oil in a large, heavy-based saucepan, add the leek and garlic and cook over a moderate heat for 5–6 minutes until the leek is softened.

2 Add the lentils, stock and herbs and bring to the boil. Reduce the heat and simmer for 10 minutes. Add the peas and cook for a further 5 minutes.

3 In a blender or food processor, blend half of the soup until smooth. Return to the pan. Reheat gently and season well with pepper.

4 Stir the crème fraîche and mint together. Ladle the soup into warm soup bowls and serve, each portion garnished with a dollop of the minty crème fraîche.

10

PREP

25

COOK

4

SERVES

herby

1 teaspoon **olive oil**

1 **leek**, thinly sliced

1 **garlic clove**, crushed

400 g (13 oz) can **Puy lentils**, drained

1.2 litres (2 pints) **Vegetable Stock** (see page 19)

2 tablespoons chopped **mixed herbs**, such as thyme and parsley

200 g (7 oz) frozen **peas**

pepper

TO GARNISH:

2 tablespoons light **crème fraîche**

1 tablespoon chopped **mint**

3 tablespoons **olive oil**

4 large **onions**, finely chopped

1.2 litres (2 pints) **Vegetable Stock** (see page 19)

2 teaspoons chopped **thyme**

1 tablespoon chopped **parsley**

salt and **pepper**

GARLIC CROÛTONS:

8–12 thick slices of French or Italian **bread**

1 small **garlic clove**, halved

2 tablespoons **olive oil**

2 tablespoons grated **Parmesan cheese** or **Cheddar cheese**

20

PREP

60

COOK

4

SERVES

classic

Onion soup with garlic croûtons

A slowly cooked onion soup is warming and uplifting in the middle of winter. The onions cook to a sweet, caramelized flavour, and the allium connection is maintained by serving the soup with garlic croûtons.

1 Heat the oil in a large, heavy-based saucepan, add the onions and cook over a low to moderate heat, stirring occasionally, for 20 minutes or until soft and golden brown.

2 Add the stock and thyme and bring to the boil. Boil for 2 minutes, then reduce the heat, cover and simmer for 30 minutes. Season to taste with salt and pepper.

3 In a blender or food processor, blend the soup in batches until smooth. Return to the pan. Reheat gently and add the parsley.

4 Meanwhile, make the croûtons. Lay the slices of bread on a baking sheet and toast under a preheated moderate grill until golden brown. Rub the top of each slice with the cut side of the garlic clove. Drizzle with the oil and sprinkle with the grated cheese.

5 Cook the bread under the grill until the cheese just begins to melt. Serve the soup in warm bowls, with the croûtons separately, or float them on top of each bowl.

White onion soup

This soup makes the most of the intense flavour and bite of Spanish onions. They are cooked slowly, with milk and cream adding a contrasting texture.

5

PREP

35

COOK

6

SERVES

easy

50 g (2 oz) **butter**

6 Spanish **onions**, thickly sliced

1 tablespoon **plain flour**

300 ml (½ pint) boiling **water**

1 litre (1¾ pints) warm **milk**

1 tablespoon **single cream**

salt and **white pepper**

1 Melt the butter in a large, heavy-based saucepan, add the onions and cook over a high heat, stirring constantly, for 3 minutes without browning. Stir in the flour and cook, stirring constantly, for 1 minute. Gradually stir in the measured boiling water.

2 Season to taste with salt and pepper. Cook over a moderate heat, stirring occasionally, for 10 minutes.

3 Gradually add the milk to the pan, stirring constantly, then cover and simmer gently for 15–20 minutes or until the onions are very tender. Taste and adjust the seasoning if necessary. Stir in the cream and serve in warm soup bowls.

25 g (1 oz) **butter**

250 g (8 oz) **spring onions**, finely chopped

3 tablespoons **plain flour**

1.2 litres (2 pints) **Vegetable Stock** (see page 19)

1 tablespoon chopped **basil**

pinch of **grated nutmeg**

150 ml (¼ pint) **single cream**

salt and **pepper**

1 tablespoon finely chopped **spring onion tops**, to garnish

10

PREP

20

COOK

4

SERVES

quick

Spring onion soup

This is an amazingly quick and easy recipe to prepare. If you like onion soup, it makes a great alternative for a change. The soup isn't blended, so it offers an interesting bite from the onions.

1 Heat the butter in a large, heavy-based saucepan, add the spring onions and cook over a moderate heat for about 5 minutes or until softened.

2 Sprinkle in the flour and cook, stirring constantly, for 1 minute. Gradually add the stock, whisking vigorously. Add the basil and nutmeg. Season to taste with salt and pepper. Simmer, stirring frequently, for 10 minutes or until slightly thickened.

3 Stir in the cream and heat through gently without boiling. Serve the soup immediately in warm bowls, garnishing each portion with a sprinkling of spring onion tops.

Truffled leek and potato soup

A drizzle of luxurious truffle oil transforms this simple soup into something very special. Truffles are prized among all fungi for their intense flavour and aroma – and although the oil is expensive, you need only a little drizzle and the taste is sublime.

1 Heat the butter in a saucepan, add the onion, garlic and leeks and cook over a moderate heat for 5 minutes. Stir in the potatoes and stock. Season to taste with salt and pepper. Bring to the boil, then reduce the heat, cover and simmer for 20 minutes.

2 In a blender or food processor, blend the soup in batches until really smooth, then return it to the pan. Reheat gently and taste and adjust the seasoning if necessary. Serve the soup in warm soup bowls, drizzled with truffle oil and sprinkled with snipped chives.

10

PREP

30

COOK

4

SERVES

posh

50 g (2 oz) **butter**

1 **onion**, chopped

1 **garlic clove**, crushed

3 **leeks**, about 375 g (12 oz) trimmed weight, sliced

300 g (10 oz) **potatoes**, diced

900 ml (1½ pints) **Vegetable Stock** (see page 19)

salt and **pepper**

TO GARNISH:

truffle oil

snipped **chives**

Pasta in broth

PREP 10

COOK 20

SERVES 4

simple

2 tablespoons **olive oil**

1 small **onion**, finely chopped

1 **celery stick**, finely chopped

several sprigs of **thyme**

1 small glass of **white wine**

1.5 litres (2½ pints) **Vegetable**, **Chicken** or **Beef Stock** (see pages 17–19)

200 g (7 oz) fresh **ravioli**, **tortellini** or **cappelletti**

2–3 tablespoons finely chopped **parsley** or **basil**

salt and **pepper**

grated or shaved **Parmesan cheese**, to serve

Pasta cooked in broth can be as simple or as elaborate as you like. Use your own specially made stuffed meat or cheese pasta, or cheat and buy ready made for a speedy supper dish.

1 Heat the oil in a large saucepan and fry the onion, celery and thyme over a gentle heat for 5 minutes.

2 Add the wine and stock and bring slowly to the boil. Reduce the heat and cook gently, uncovered, for 5 minutes.

3 Return the broth to the boil and drop in the pasta. Cook for 5 minutes. Test by lifting out one piece and cutting it in half. The pasta should be just tender and the filling cooked through.

4 Stir in the parsley or basil and season to taste with salt and pepper. Ladle the broth into warm bowls and serve sprinkled with plenty of Parmesan.

Garlic soup with a floating egg

This soup is based on a Spanish dish in which the eggs are poached or oven-baked in a rich, garlicky broth. Here, pasta is added to give a little more substance to the dish.

5

PREP

15

COOK

4

SERVES

stylish

1 Heat the oil in a large, heavy-based saucepan, add the bread slices and cook over a moderate heat, turning once, until golden. Remove with a slotted spoon and drain on kitchen paper.

2 Add the garlic, onion, paprika and cumin to the pan and cook, stirring, for 3 minutes. Add the saffron and stock and bring to the boil. Stir in the pasta, then reduce the heat, cover and simmer for 8 minutes or until the pasta is just tender. Season to taste with salt and pepper.

3 Break the eggs on to a saucer and slide them into the pan, one at a time. Cook for 2–3 minutes until poached.

4 Stack 3 slices of fried bread in each of 4 soup bowls. Ladle the soup over the bread, making sure each serving contains an egg. Serve immediately.

4 tablespoons **olive oil**

12 thick slices of **baguette**

5 **garlic cloves**, sliced

1 **onion**, finely chopped

1 tablespoon **paprika**

1 teaspoon **ground cumin**

good pinch of **saffron threads**

1.2 litres (2 pints) **Vegetable Stock** (see page 19)

25 g (1 oz) dried soup **pasta**

4 **eggs**

salt and **pepper**

4 tablespoons **olive oil**

375 g (12 oz) **shallots**, sliced

1 **red onion**, roughly chopped

2 **garlic cloves**, roughly chopped

4 large sprigs of **rosemary**

1 teaspoon **caster sugar**

750 ml (1¼ pints) **Vegetable Stock** (see page 19)

5 tablespoons **double cream**

salt and **pepper**

toasted French bread **croûtons**, to serve

PREP 10

COOK 20

SERVES 4

herby

Shallot and rosemary soup

This smooth soup makes a good stand-by for vegetarian suppers. If you don't want to make croûtons, serve this with plenty of crusty French bread.

1 Heat the oil in a saucepan, add the shallots, onion, garlic, rosemary and sugar and cook over a moderate heat for 5 minutes or until softened and lightly browned.

2 Add the stock and bring to the boil. Reduce the heat, cover and simmer gently for about 15 minutes until the shallots are tender.

3 In a blender or food processor, blend the soup in batches until smooth, then return it to the pan.

4 Stir in the cream and season to taste with salt and pepper. Reheat gently for 1 minute, then ladle the soup into warm soup bowls and serve sprinkled with croûtons.

Courgette soup

10
PREP

30
COOK

This soup, which couldn't be easier to make, is delicious served cold in summer, as the lemon gives it a really fresh clean taste.

4
SERVES

fresh

2 tablespoons **olive oil**

4 **shallots**, diced

1 **garlic clove**, crushed

6 **courgettes**, diced

2 **potatoes**, chopped

1.2 litres (2 pints) **Chicken Stock** (see page 17)

75 g (3 oz) **farfallini** or other small pasta shapes

juice and rind of 1 **lemon**

large handful of **chives**, snipped

salt and **pepper**

1 Heat the oil in a large, heavy-based saucepan, add the shallots and garlic and cook over a moderate heat for 3 minutes.

2 Add the courgettes, potatoes and stock and bring to the boil. Reduce the heat and simmer for 15 minutes.

3 In a blender or food processor, blend the soup in batches until smooth, or press it through a sieve, then return it to the pan.

4 Add the pasta and simmer for 7 minutes or until just tender. Stir in the lemon rind and juice and chives, then season to taste with salt and pepper. Serve the soup immediately in warm soup bowls.

25 g (1 oz) **butter**

1 tablespoon **olive oil**

1 large **onion**, chopped

475 g (15 oz) **courgettes**, sliced

75 g (3 oz) **pine nuts**

1 tablespoon chopped **sage**

1 litre (1¾ pints) **Vegetable Stock** (see page 19)

100 g (3½) oz **Parmesan cheese**, crumbled

4 tablespoons **double cream**

salt and **pepper**

10

PREP

15

COOK

4

SERVES

quick

Courgette and Parmesan soup

It's worth buying a good-quality Parmesan for this recipe, as it's a key ingredient. The Italian theme continues with the pine nuts, which are usually toasted or fried to bring out their flavour.

1 Melt the butter with the oil in a large, heavy-based saucepan, add the onion, courgettes and pine nuts and cook over a moderate heat for 5 minutes or until softened.

2 Add the sage and stock and bring to the boil, then reduce the heat, cover and simmer gently for 5 minutes. Add the Parmesan and cook for a further 2 minutes.

3 In a blender or food processor, blend the soup in batches until partially blended but not smooth, then return it to the pan.

4 Stir in the cream and season to taste with salt and pepper. Reheat gently for 1 minute, then serve in warm soup bowls.

Courgette soup with fresh ginger

Fresh root ginger, so popular in oriental cooking, livens up the flavour of this soup, which would otherwise be dominated by the slight blandness of the courgettes.

20* PREP

55 COOK

6 SERVES

tasty

1.5 kg (3 lb) small **courgettes**

50 g (2 oz) **butter**

250 g (8 oz) **onions**, chopped

1 litre (1¾ pints) **Vegetable Stock** (see page 19)

1 tablespoon grated fresh **root ginger**

pinch of **grated nutmeg**

375 g (12 oz) **potatoes**, chopped

salt and **pepper**

150 ml (¼ pint) **single cream**, to serve

1 Trim the courgettes and slice thickly into a colander. Sprinkle with salt and leave to drain for 10–15 minutes. Rinse under cold running water, drain thoroughly and pat dry with kitchen paper.

2 Melt the butter in a large, heavy-based saucepan, add the onions and cook over a moderate heat for 5 minutes or until softened. Add the courgettes and cook over a low heat, stirring frequently, for 5 minutes.

3 Add the stock, ginger and nutmeg and season to taste with pepper. Bring to the boil and add the potatoes, then reduce the heat, partially cover and simmer for about 40–45 minutes until the vegetables are tender.

4 In a blender or food processor, blend the soup in batches until smooth, then transfer it to a clean saucepan. Reheat gently, then serve in warm soup bowls with a swirl of cream on each portion.

* Plus 10–15 minutes draining

25 g (1 oz) **butter**

1 large **onion**, finely chopped

425 g (14 oz) frozen **peas**

2 **Little Gem lettuces**, roughly chopped

1 litre (1¾ pints) **Vegetable Stock** (see page 19)

grated rind and juice of ½ **lemon**

salt and **pepper**

SESAME CROÛTONS:

2 thick slices of **bread**, cut into cubes

1 tablespoon **olive oil**

1 tablespoon **sesame seeds**

PREP 10

25 COOK

4 SERVES

light

Pea, lettuce and lemon soup

Lettuce might seem an unusual ingredient for a soup, but it's actually very good cooked. This is a light, refreshing soup that would be ideal for a summer lunch.

1 Make the croûtons. Brush the bread cubes with the oil and spread out in a roasting tin. Sprinkle with the sesame seeds and bake in a preheated oven, 200°C (400°F), Gas Mark 6, for 10–15 minutes or until golden.

2 Meanwhile, melt the butter in a large, heavy-based saucepan, add the onion and cook over a moderate heat for 5 minutes or until softened. Add the peas, lettuce, stock, lemon rind and juice and salt and pepper to taste. Bring to the boil, then reduce the heat, cover and simmer for 10–15 minutes.

3 In a blender or food processor, blend the soup in batches until smooth, then return it to the pan. Taste and adjust the seasoning if necessary. Reheat gently. Ladle into warm soup bowls and serve sprinkled with the sesame croûtons.

Pea and mint soup

Mint is one of the easiest herbs to grow, whether you have space for plants in your garden borders or room on a balcony or by the back door for a single container. Use the fresh leaves all year round in salads or as a garnish, or, as here, in a summery soup.

1 Melt the butter in a large, heavy-based saucepan, add the onion and cook over a moderate heat for 5 minutes or until softened.

2 Add the peas, sugar, stock and 3 tablespoons of the chopped mint. Add pepper to taste and bring to the boil. Add the potatoes, then reduce the heat, partially cover and simmer for 20–25 minutes.

3 In a blender or food processor, blend the soup in batches, then transfer it to a clean saucepan. Season to taste with salt, add the cream and stir well. Reheat gently without boiling. Serve in warm soup bowls, garnished with the remaining mint.

10
PREP

35
COOK

6
SERVES

classic

50 g (2 oz) **butter**

1 small **onion**, chopped

500 g (1 lb) frozen **peas**

¼ teaspoon **caster sugar**

1.2 litres (2 pints) **Vegetable Stock** (see page 19)

4 tablespoons chopped **mint**

300 g (10 oz) **potatoes**, roughly chopped

150 ml (¼ pint) **double cream**

salt and **white pepper**

50 g (2 oz) **butter**

500 g (1 lb) **cucumbers**, peeled, deseeded and cut into 1 cm (½ inch) pieces

250 g (8 oz) **peas**, fresh or frozen

pinch of **caster sugar**

¼ teaspoon **white pepper**

3 tablespoons finely chopped **mint**

1.2 litres (2 pints) **Vegetable Stock** (see page 19)

175 g (6 oz) **potatoes**, chopped

150 ml (¼ pint) **double cream**

salt

15*

PREP

30

COOK

6

SERVES

fresh

Mint, cucumber and green pea soup

There's a strong green theme in this tasty summer soup. Opt for fresh peas in the pod, as part of the fun is shelling them. Mint is the perfect partner for peas, and the cucumbers give a light, fresh flavour.

1 Heat the butter in a large, heavy-based saucepan, add the cucumber and cook over a moderate heat for 5 minutes. Add the peas, sugar, pepper and 2 tablespoons of the mint. Pour in the stock and bring to the boil, then add the potatoes. Reduce the heat, partially cover and simmer for 20 minutes or until the potatoes are tender.

2 In a blender or food processor, blend the soup in batches until smooth, then transfer it to a clean saucepan or, if it is to be served cold, to a bowl. Season to taste with salt.

3 If the soup is to be served hot, add the cream and reheat gently without boiling. Serve in warm soup bowls, garnishing each portion with a little of the remaining mint.

4 If the soup is to be served cold, cover the bowl closely and chill for at least 3 hours, making sure that the cream is also chilled. Just before serving, fold in the chilled cream. Serve in chilled bowls, garnishing each portion with some of the remaining mint.

* Plus 3 hours chilling if served cold

Sweet potato and coconut soup

This rich, filling soup is ideal for a weekend lunch. If you cannot find a whole coconut, instead of the homemade coconut milk, you can use 600 ml (1 pint) water and a 400 ml (14 fl oz) can of coconut milk instead.

1 Drill holes in the 3 coconut eyes. Pour out the liquid and reserve. Crack the coconut open, prise out the flesh and grate roughly.

2 Put the grated coconut in a heatproof bowl with the measured boiling water and leave to stand for 1 hour. Squeeze and rub the grated coconut into the water, as if washing, to extract as much of the juice and oil from the flesh as you can. Strain the liquid into a jug. Reserve 2 tablespoons of the coconut pulp.

3 Heat the oil in a large, heavy-based saucepan, add the onions and cook over a moderate heat for 10 minutes. Add the sweet potato and cook for 5 minutes. Add the garlic, ginger, chilli flakes, reserved coconut water, white coconut milk, reserved coconut pulp and salt and pepper to taste. Bring to a fast simmer without boiling. Reduce the heat, cover and simmer for 30–35 minutes until the sweet potato is tender.

4 In a blender or food processor, blend the soup in batches, then transfer it to a clean pan. Gently reheat and serve in warm bowls.

25 *
PREP

55
COOK

4
SERVES

exotic

1 small **coconut**

1 litre (1¾ pints) boiling **water**

4 tablespoons **olive oil**

2 **onions**, finely chopped

500 g (1 lb) **sweet potatoes**, roughly chopped

2 **garlic cloves**, crushed

7 cm (3 inch) piece of fresh **root ginger**, peeled and finely chopped

¼ teaspoon dried **chilli flakes**

salt and **pepper**

* Plus 1 hour standing

500 g (1 lb) waxy **new potatoes**, such as Jersey Royals, scrubbed

3 small **leeks**

40 g (1½ oz) **butter**

1 tablespoon **black mustard seeds**

1 **onion**, chopped

1 **garlic clove**, thinly sliced

1 litre (1¾ pints) **Vegetable Stock** (see page 19)

plenty of **grated nutmeg**

small handful of fresh **coriander**, roughly chopped

salt and **pepper**

warm **bread**, to serve

10

PREP

20

COOK

4

SERVES

herby

New potato, coriander and leek soup

Leek and potato is a favourite combination for soups, but the addition of coriander gives a new twist. Chop the coriander at the last minute to keep it as fresh as possible.

1 Halve the potatoes or cut them into 1 cm (½ inch) slices if large. Halve the leeks lengthways, then cut across into thin shreds.

2 Melt the butter in a large, heavy-based saucepan, add the mustard seeds, onion, garlic and potatoes and cook over a moderate heat for 5 minutes. Add the stock and nutmeg and bring just to the boil. Reduce the heat, cover and simmer gently for 10 minutes or until the potatoes are just tender.

3 Stir in the leeks and coriander and cook for a further 5 minutes. Season to taste with salt and pepper and serve with warm bread.

Creamed corn and potato soup

This is a soup for cold winter evenings or when you're feeling a bit under the weather. The comforting combination of potato and sweetcorn is guaranteed to cheer you up.

1 Heat the oil in a large, heavy-based saucepan, add the onion and celery and cook over a moderate heat for 5 minutes. Add the stock and bring to the boil.

2 Add the potatoes, then reduce the heat and simmer, uncovered, for 5 minutes. Add the sweetcorn kernels and tarragon, cover and simmer for a further 5 minutes or until the potatoes are tender.

3 In a blender or food processor, blend the soup in batches until pulpy but not smooth, then return it to the pan.

4 Add the nutmeg and cream. Season to taste with salt and pepper. Reheat gently for 1 minute, then serve in warm soup bowls.

10
PREP

20
COOK

4
SERVES

filling

2 tablespoons **olive oil**

1 **onion**, chopped

2 **celery sticks**, thinly sliced

1 litre (1¾ pints) **Vegetable Stock** (see page 19)

400 g (13 oz) **potatoes**, diced

300 g (10 oz) frozen **sweetcorn kernels**

2 tablespoons chopped **tarragon**

plenty of **grated nutmeg**

4 tablespoons **double cream**

salt and **pepper**

50 g (2 oz) **butter**

1 small **onion**, chopped

2 **dessert apples**, peeled, cored and sliced

pinch of **cayenne pepper** (or to taste)

600 ml (1 pint) **Vegetable Stock** (see page 19)

300 g (10 oz) **potatoes**, sliced

300 ml (½ pint) hot **milk**

salt

TO GARNISH:

15 g (½ oz) **butter**

2–3 thinly sliced **dessert apple** quarters

cayenne pepper

15

PREP

30

COOK

4

SERVES

spicy

Spicy apple and potato soup

The combination of apple and potato is not an obvious one, but this soup is delicious. The cayenne pepper adds spice and contrast to the velvety smooth texture.

1 Melt the butter in a large, heavy-based saucepan, add the onion and cook over a moderate heat for 5 minutes or until softened. Add the apples and cayenne pepper and cook, stirring, for 2 minutes. Pour in the stock, then add the potatoes. Bring to the boil, then reduce the heat and simmer gently for 15–18 minutes or until the apples and potatoes are very tender.

2 In a blender or food processor, blend the soup in batches until very smooth, then transfer it to a clean saucepan. Reheat gently and stir in the hot milk. Taste and adjust the seasoning if necessary.

3 Meanwhile, make the garnish. Melt the butter in a small frying pan, add the apple and cook over a high heat until crisp. Serve the soup in warm bowls, garnishing each portion with some sliced apple and a sprinkling of cayenne pepper.

Cream of celeriac soup

Creamed soups are always a favourite. Blended vegetables work really well with the addition of milk or cream, and the pinch of freshly grated nutmeg in this recipe finishes the soup off perfectly.

1 Put the stock in a large, heavy-based saucepan with the bay leaf, nutmeg and pepper. Bring to the boil.

2 Add the celeriac and potatoes and season to taste with salt. Return to the boil, then reduce the heat, partially cover and simmer for 35 minutes or until all the vegetables are tender. Remove and discard the bay leaf.

3 In a blender or food processor, blend the soup in batches, then transfer it to a clean saucepan. Reheat gently without boiling and stir in the cream. Ladle into warm soup bowls, sprinkle each portion with finely chopped parsley and serve immediately.

15

PREP

45

COOK

4

SERVES

rich

1.2 litres (2 pints) **Vegetable Stock** (see page 19)

1 **bay leaf**

pinch of **grated nutmeg**

¼ teaspoon **white pepper**

about 750 g (1½ lb) **celeriac**, diced

375 g (12 oz) **potatoes**, diced

250 ml (8 fl oz) **single cream**

salt

finely chopped **parsley**, to garnish

50 g (2 oz) **unsalted butter**

500 g (1 lb) **celery**, sliced, leaves reserved to garnish

500 g (1 lb) **carrots**, chopped

250 g (8 oz) **dessert apples**, peeled, cored and roughly chopped

1.2 litres (2 pints) **Vegetable Stock** (see page 19)

1 teaspoon **paprika**, plus extra to garnish

cayenne pepper, to taste

1 tablespoon chopped **basil**

1 **bay leaf**

1 teaspoon grated fresh **root ginger**

salt and **white pepper**

15

PREP

60

COOK

6

SERVES

tasty

Celery, carrot and apple soup

This interesting combination of ingredients blends together surprisingly well. The herbs and spices add colour, fragrant flavour and a little heat.

1 Melt the butter in a large, heavy-based saucepan and add the celery, carrots and apple. Cover tightly and cook over a low heat, stirring occasionally, for 15 minutes.

2 Add the stock, paprika, cayenne pepper, basil, bay leaf and ginger. Bring to the boil, then reduce the heat, partially cover and simmer for about 40–45 minutes until the vegetables and apple are tender.

3 In a blender or food processor, blend the soup in batches until smooth, then transfer it to a bowl. Press through a sieve into a clean saucepan, then season to taste with salt and pepper. Reheat gently. Ladle into warm soup bowls, and serve immediately, garnishing each portion with finely chopped celery leaves and a light sprinkling of paprika.

Cream of celery and leek soup

Cooked celery has quite a strong flavour and tastes quite different from raw celery. It is used here with leeks, and little else is required to flavour the soup.

15

PREP

60

COOK

6

SERVES

thick

50 g (2 oz) **butter**

500 g (1 lb) **celery**, sliced, leaves reserved to garnish

250 g (8 oz) **leeks**, white parts only, sliced

1.2 litres (2 pints) **Vegetable Stock** (see page 19)

1 sprig of **parsley**

1 **bay leaf**

150 ml (¼ pint) **double cream**

salt and **white pepper**

1 Melt the butter in a large, heavy-based saucepan and add the celery and leeks. Cover tightly and cook over a low heat, stirring occasionally, for 15 minutes.

2 Add the stock, parsley and bay leaf. Bring to the boil, then reduce the heat, partially cover and simmer for 40–45 minutes. Remove and discard the parsley and bay leaf.

3 In a blender or food processor, blend the soup in batches until smooth, then transfer it to a bowl. Press through a sieve into a clean saucepan, then season to taste with salt and pepper. Reheat gently without boiling. Stir in the cream, then serve immediately in warm soup bowls, garnishing each portion with finely chopped celery leaves.

PESTO:

3 **garlic cloves**, crushed

handful of **basil**

2 tablespoons **pine nuts**

50 g (2 oz) **Parmesan cheese**, grated

3 tablespoons **olive oil**

SOUP:

3 tablespoons **olive oil**

1 **onion**, diced

2 **leeks**, sliced

1 **potato**, chopped

425 g (14 oz) can **haricot beans**, rinsed and drained

1.5 litres (2½ pints) **Vegetable Stock** (see page 19)

2 **courgettes**, diced

125 g (4 oz) small **green beans**, cut into small pieces

125 g (4 oz) **broccoli** florets, chopped

250 g (8 oz) can **artichoke hearts**

1 tablespoon **flat leaf parsley**, chopped

salt and **pepper**

20

PREP

20

COOK

4

SERVES

fresh

Pesto and vegetable soup

Homemade pesto is easy to make, and you could also use this version as a pasta sauce. The wonderful array of vegetables results in a colourful soup that's packed full of vitamins and minerals. Serve it with warm focaccia bread for a substantial meal.

1 Make the pesto. In a blender or food processor, blend the garlic, basil, pine nuts and Parmesan thoroughly. Add the oil and blend again. Set aside.

2 Heat the oil for the soup in a large, heavy-based saucepan, add the onion and leeks and cook over a moderate heat for 3 minutes.

3 Add the potato, haricot beans and stock and season to taste with salt and pepper. Bring to the boil, then reduce the heat and simmer for 12 minutes.

4 Add the courgettes, green beans, broccoli and artichoke hearts to the pan and simmer for 5 minutes.

5 Add the parsley and pesto and stir well. Serve immediately in warm soup bowls.

Chilli and pimiento soup

10
PREP

The fresh red chilli gives this soup a bit of a punch, and it would be good to serve as a starter to a Mexican meal. Serve the soup with some tortilla chips for dunking.

15
COOK

1 Heat the oil in a large, heavy-based saucepan, add the onions, garlic and chilli and cook over a moderate heat for 3 minutes.

2 Add the pimientos, tomatoes, sugar and stock and bring to the boil. Reduce the heat, cover and simmer gently for 10 minutes or until the tomatoes are tender.

4
SERVES

3 In a blender or food processor, blend the soup in batches until smooth, then return it to the pan. Stir in the coriander and crème fraîche, then season to taste with salt and pepper. Reheat gently for 1 minute, then serve in warm soup bowls.

hot

2 tablespoons **olive oil**

2 **onions**, chopped

2 **garlic cloves**, chopped

1 **red chilli**, deseeded and sliced

200 g (7 oz) jar **pimientos**, drained

500 g (1 lb) **tomatoes**, skinned

2 teaspoons **caster sugar**

1 litre (1¾ pints) **Vegetable Stock** (see page 19)

2 tablespoons chopped fresh **coriander**

4 tablespoons **crème fraîche**

salt and **pepper**

40 g (1½ oz) **ghee** or **butter**

1 **onion**, chopped

2 **garlic cloves**, crushed

2 teaspoons grated fresh **root ginger**

1 large **potato**, diced

1 large **carrot**, diced

2 teaspoons **ground coriander**

1 teaspoon **ground cumin**

½ teaspoon **garam masala**

125 g (4 oz) **red lentils**, washed and drained

600 ml (1 pint) **Vegetable Stock** (see page 19)

600 ml (1 pint) **tomato juice**

salt and **pepper**

TO SERVE:

raita

naan bread

15 PREP

35 COOK

4 SERVES

hearty

Curried vegetable soup

This warming and satisfying dish is ideal for cold winter nights. Ghee, traditionally used in Indian cooking for shallow-frying, is rather similar to clarified butter. You can often find it in cans in larger supermarkets or seek it out in a specialist Indian food store.

1 Melt the ghee or butter in a large, heavy-based saucepan, add the onion, garlic, ginger, potato and carrot and cook over a moderate heat for 10 minutes. Stir in the spices and then add all the remaining ingredients.

2 Bring to the boil, then reduce the heat, cover and simmer gently for 20–25 minutes or until the lentils and vegetables are tender.

3 Season to taste with salt and pepper, then spoon the soup into warm bowls. Top each bowl with a spoonful of raita and serve with naan bread.

Walnut soup

This intense, rich soup, which is made with toasted and ground walnuts, can be found all over the Middle East and also in North Africa, where nuts are widely used in cooking.

1 Heat the oil in a large, heavy-based saucepan, add the onion, garlic, cinnamon, cumin and coriander and cook, stirring frequently, for 5 minutes or until lightly golden. Add the walnuts and breadcrumbs and cook, stirring occasionally, for a further 5 minutes.

2 In a blender or food processor, blend the onion and spice mixture with a spoonful of the stock, the lemon juice and pomegranate syrup to form a paste. Gradually blend in the remaining stock.

3 Return the mixture to the saucepan and bring slowly to the boil. Reduce the heat, cover and simmer for 15 minutes. Season to taste with salt and pepper. Serve in warm soup bowls topped with a spoonful of Greek yogurt and a drizzle of chilli oil.

15
PREP

25
COOK

6
SERVES

stylish

4 tablespoons **walnut oil** or **olive oil**

1 **onion**, finely chopped

1 **garlic clove**, crushed

1 teaspoon **ground cinnamon**

¼ teaspoon **ground cumin**

¼ teaspoon **ground coriander**

175 g (6 oz) **walnuts**, toasted and chopped

50 g (2 oz) dry **breadcrumbs**

1 litre (1¾ pints) **Vegetable Stock** (see page 19)

1 tablespoon **lemon juice**

1 tablespoon **pomegranate syrup**

salt and **pepper**

TO SERVE:

Greek yogurt

chilli oil

375 g (12 oz) **Jerusalem artichokes** or **Chinese artichokes**, scrubbed

25 g (1 oz) **butter**, melted

1 tablespoon **olive oil**

1 **onion**, finely chopped

1 sprig of **thyme**

600 ml (1 pint) **Vegetable Stock** (see page 19)

150 ml (¼ pint) **double cream**

salt and **pepper**

large thick bread **croûtons**, to serve

SALSA DULCE:

1 **garlic clove**

25 g (1 oz) dry **breadcrumbs**

1 tablespoon chopped **flat leaf parsley**

1 tablespoon chopped **dill**

1 tablespoon chopped **tarragon**

1 small **red pepper**, cored, deseeded and finely chopped

3 tablespoons **olive oil**

15

PREP

50

COOK

4

SERVES

exotic

Roasted artichoke soup

You can use Jerusalem or Chinese artichokes in this soup. Roasting them contributes a slightly smoky flavour to the soup, while the salsa dulce, made with green herbs and sweet red pepper, adds a dash of colour and a punch of aroma. The salsa is stirred into the soup just before eating.

1 Cut the Jerusalem artichokes in half if they are large. Put in a small roasting tin and drizzle over the melted butter. Sprinkle with salt and pepper to taste. Roast in a preheated oven, 200°C (400°F), Gas Mark 6, for 30 minutes (10 minutes for Chinese artichokes) or until cooked through and lightly browned.

2 Heat the oil in a large, heavy-based saucepan, add the onion and cook over a moderate heat for 5 minutes. Add the roasted artichokes, thyme and stock and bring to a gentle boil. Reduce the heat and simmer for 10 minutes. Add salt and pepper to taste.

3 Meanwhile, make the salsa. In a blender or food processor, blend the garlic, breadcrumbs and herbs until finely chopped. Add the red pepper, oil and salt and pepper to taste and blend to a coarse purée. Set aside.

4 In the blender or food processor, blend the soup in batches until smooth, then return it to the pan. Reheat gently, then add the cream. Serve in warm soup bowls, each serving topped with a croûton and a spoonful of salsa.

Jerusalem artichoke soup

15

PREP

40

COOK

6

SERVES

rich

The Jerusalem artichoke received its name through inaccurate description and incorrect pronunciation, since it has nothing to do with an artichoke or with Jerusalem. These tubers were originally grown by native Americans and were discovered in 1605 by French explorers in Massachusetts.

1 If the artichokes are fairly smooth, peel and drop immediately into acidulated water (with lemon juice) to prevent discoloration. If they are knobbly, scrub in plenty of water and cut off the dark tips and any small, dry roots. Slice the artichokes and drop immediately into acidulated water.

2 Melt the butter in a large, heavy-based saucepan, add the onion and cook over a moderate heat for 5 minutes or until softened. Add the artichokes and cook, stirring, for 3 minutes. Season to taste with salt and pepper. Add the stock and milk. Bring to simmering point, stirring constantly. Reduce the heat, partially cover and simmer for 30 minutes or until the vegetables are tender.

3 In a blender or food processor, blend the soup briefly in batches, then transfer it to a clean saucepan. Reheat gently without boiling, then add the cream. Serve in warm soup bowls, garnished with finely chopped parsley and croûtons.

1 kg (2 lb) **Jerusalem artichokes**

lemon juice

50 g (2 oz) **butter**

1 **onion**, chopped

600 ml (1 pint) **Vegetable Stock** (see page 19)

600 ml (1 pint) **milk**

150 ml (¼ pint) **single cream**

salt and **white pepper**

TO GARNISH:

finely chopped **parsley**

croûtons

50 g (2 oz) **butter**

1 **onion**, chopped

1 **garlic clove**, chopped

1 **celery stick**, sliced

425 g (14 oz) can
artichoke hearts,
drained

1.2 litres (2 pints)
Vegetable Stock
(see page 19)

1 tablespoon **lemon juice**

3 tablespoons chopped
dill

2 tablespoons **plain flour**

150 ml (¼ pint) **single
cream**

salt and **white pepper**

4–6 sprigs of **dill**, to
garnish

20

PREP

35

COOK

4

SERVES

posh

Heart of artichoke soup with dill

Dill has a distinctive taste, and is often used with fish, such as salmon. Here, it works well with the tender artichoke hearts. This is a good soup for entertaining.

1 Melt the butter in a large, heavy-based saucepan and add the onion, garlic and celery. Cover and cook over a moderate heat, stirring occasionally, for 10–12 minutes or until all the vegetables are tender.

2 Add the artichoke hearts, cover and cook for a further 3 minutes. Pour in 1 litre (1¾ pints) of the stock and the lemon juice. Stir in 1 tablespoon of the dill. Cover and simmer for 15 minutes.

3 In a blender or food processor, blend the soup in batches until smooth, transferring to a clean saucepan.

4 In a small bowl, blend the flour with the remaining stock, adding a little water if necessary. Reheat the soup, whisk in the flour mixture and cook, stirring constantly, until slightly thickened. Add the remaining dill and season to taste with salt and pepper, then add the cream. Heat thoroughly without boiling. Serve the soup in warm soup bowls, garnishing each portion with a dill sprig.

Watercress and apple soup

15
PREP

30
COOK

Watercress is usually confined to salads, but it makes a really good soup, especially when it's combined with cream. Dessert apples aren't as sweet as eating apples, so they're ideal for savoury dishes.

4
SERVES

1 Melt the butter in a large, heavy-based saucepan, add the watercress and apples and cook over a moderate heat for 3–5 minutes. Stir in the stock, potatoes, lemon juice and nutmeg and season to taste with salt and pepper. Bring to the boil, then reduce the heat, cover and simmer for 15–20 minutes or until the apples and potatoes are tender.

2 In a blender or food processor, blend the soup in batches until smooth, then transfer it to a clean saucepan. Add the cream and gently reheat without boiling. Serve the soup in warm soup bowls, garnishing each portion with a sprinkling of the finely chopped apple.

light

50 g (2 oz) **butter**

2 bunches of **watercress**, stalks discarded, roughly chopped

125 g (4 oz) peeled, cored and chopped **dessert apples**

1 litre (1¾ pints) **Vegetable Stock** (see page 19)

250 g (8 oz) **potatoes**, chopped

1 teaspoon **lemon juice**

pinch of **grated nutmeg**

150 ml (¼ pint) **single cream**, chilled

salt and **pepper**

1 tablespoon finely chopped **dessert apple**, to garnish

50 g (2 oz) **butter**

1 **onion**, chopped

1 **celery stick**, sliced

1 large **cauliflower**,
about 750 g (1½ lb), cut
into small florets

600 ml (1 pint)
Vegetable Stock
(see page 19)

900 ml (1½ pints) **milk**

1 teaspoon **grated
nutmeg**

1 tablespoon **cornflour**

250 g (8 oz) **Stilton
cheese**, crumbled

125 ml (4 fl oz) **double
cream**

salt and **white pepper**

finely chopped **parsley**,
to garnish

15

PREP

35

COOK

6

SERVES

filling

Cauliflower soup with Stilton

Cauliflower is a versatile vegetable that can be transformed into a variety of flavoursome soups. Cheese is a delicious accompaniment.

1 Melt the butter in a large, heavy-based saucepan and add the onion, celery and cauliflower. Cover and cook over a moderate heat, stirring frequently, for 5–8 minutes. Stir in the stock with 450 ml (¾ pint) of the milk. Bring to the boil, then reduce the heat, cover and simmer for 25 minutes.

2 In a blender or food processor, blend the soup in batches until smooth, then transfer it to a clean saucepan. Stir in 300 ml (½ pint) of the remaining milk. Season to taste with salt and pepper and stir in the nutmeg.

3 In a small bowl, blend the cornflour with the remaining milk and add to the soup. Bring to the boil, stirring constantly. Reduce the heat and simmer for 2 minutes. Stir in the Stilton and cream. Heat through gently without boiling, stirring constantly. Serve immediately in warm soup bowls, garnished with a sprinkling of finely chopped parsley.

Carrot soup

15

PREP

40

COOK

The humble, versatile carrot with its bright colour and sweetish flavour can be used in a variety of delicious soups.

6

SERVES

1 Melt the butter in a large, heavy-based saucepan, add the onion and cook over a moderate heat for 5 minutes or until softened. Add the carrots and turnips and cook, stirring constantly, for 1 minute. Pour in the measured water and the stock. Stir, then add the potatoes and sugar. Season to taste with salt and pepper. Bring to the boil. Reduce the heat, cover and simmer for 25–30 minutes.

2 In a blender or food processor, blend the soup in batches until smooth, then transfer it to a clean saucepan.

3 Reheat gently without boiling. Taste and adjust the seasoning if necessary. Just before serving, stir in the cream, if liked. Serve in warm soup bowls.

simple

50 g (2 oz) **butter**

1 **onion**, chopped

500 g (1 lb) **carrots**, sliced

2 **turnips**, diced

900 ml (1½ pints) **water**

600 ml (1 pint) **Vegetable Stock** (see page 19)

250 g (8 oz) **potatoes**, sliced

pinch of **caster sugar**

3 tablespoons **double cream** (optional)

salt and **pepper**

50 g (2 oz) **butter**

1 **onion**, chopped

500 g (1 lb) **carrots**, sliced

2 **turnips**, diced

900 ml (1½ pints) **water**

600 ml (1 pint) **Vegetable Stock** (see page 19)

250 g (8 oz) **potatoes**, sliced

pinch of **caster sugar**

2–3 tablespoons mild **curry powder**

½ teaspoon **ground cumin**

½ teaspoon **ground turmeric**

150 ml (¼ pint) **double cream**

salt and **pepper**

15

PREP

40

COOK

6

SERVES

spicy

Creamy curried carrot soup

This is an easy-to-cook variation of the basic Carrot Soup (see page 141). It's ideal for a quick midweek supper and delicious served with warm crusty bread or naan bread.

1 Melt the butter in a large, heavy-based saucepan, add the onion and cook over a moderate heat for 5 minutes until softened. Add the carrots and turnips and cook, stirring constantly, for 1 minute. Pour in the measured water and the stock. Stir, then add the potatoes and sugar. Season to taste with salt and pepper. Add the curry powder, cumin and turmeric. Bring to the boil. Reduce the heat, cover and simmer for 25–30 minutes.

2 In a blender or food processor, blend the soup in batches until smooth, then transfer it to a clean saucepan.

3 Add the cream and reheat gently without boiling. Taste and adjust the seasoning if necessary. Serve in warm soup bowls.

Cream of asparagus soup

Save this recipe for when fresh asparagus is in season. This is a simple soup that relies on the quality of its ingredients to make it shine.

10

PREP

30

COOK

6

SERVES

classic

1 kg (2 lb) **asparagus**

2 litres (3½ pints) **water**

25 g (1 oz) **butter**

1 tablespoon **plain flour**

pinch of **grated nutmeg**

2 **egg yolks**

300 ml (½ pint) **double cream**

salt and **white pepper**

1 tablespoon snipped **chives**, to garnish

1 Trim the ends of the asparagus and cut the spears into 2.5 cm (1 inch) segments. Bring the measured water, lightly salted, to the boil, add the asparagus and cook for 15 minutes or until very tender. Drain, reserving the liquid in a jug.

2 Melt the butter in a large, heavy-based saucepan, stir in the flour and cook over a moderate heat, stirring constantly, for 1 minute. Gradually add the reserved liquid, bring to the boil, stirring constantly, and cook until thickened. Add the nutmeg and salt and pepper to taste and cook, stirring frequently, for a further 3–5 minutes.

3 Add the asparagus and reduce the heat. Simmer gently, stirring occasionally, for a further 5 minutes.

4 In a small bowl, beat the egg yolks with the cream and add a little pepper. Pour into the soup. Stir well and cook for a further 1 minute without boiling. Serve in warm soup bowls, garnishing each portion with a sprinkling of snipped chives.

1 tablespoon **olive oil**

50 g (2 oz) rindless unsmoked **streaky bacon**, finely chopped

1 **onion**, chopped

1 **celery stick**, thinly sliced

375 g (12 oz) **Brussels sprouts**, trimmed and chopped

900 ml (1½ pints) **water**

375 g (12 oz) **potatoes**, cut into 1 cm (½ inch) cubes

1 teaspoon finely chopped **marjoram**

pinch of **grated nutmeg** (or to taste)

1 **egg yolk**

4 tablespoons **milk**

salt and **white pepper**

15

PREP

50

COOK

6

SERVES

hearty

Brussels sprouts soup

Brussels sprouts don't tend to feature on many people's list of favourite vegetables, and this is a great way to disguise them! Once people have complimented you on the soup, they might change their minds.

1 Heat the oil in a large, heavy-based saucepan, add the bacon and cook over a moderate heat or 5 minutes or until golden. Add the onion and celery, cover and cook, stirring frequently, for 5 minutes. Add the Brussels sprouts and cook for 5–8 minutes.

2 Stir in the measured water, potatoes, marjoram and nutmeg and bring to the boil. Reduce the heat and simmer, uncovered, for 30 minutes or until the potatoes are tender. Season to taste with salt and pepper.

3 In a blender or food processor, blend the the soup in batches until smooth, then transfer it to a clean saucepan.

4 In a small bowl, beat the egg yolk with the milk. Bring the soup to simmering point, then stir in the egg and milk mixture and heat through without boiling. Serve the soup immediately in warm soup bowls.

Kale soup with garlic croûtons

Garlic croûtons provide a crisp counterpoint to this soup. They can be made in advance and stored in the refrigerator in an airtight container. To reheat, spread the croûtons on a baking sheet and place in a very hot oven for a few minutes.

1 Melt the butter in a large saucepan, add the onion and cook over a moderate heat for 5 minutes or until softened. Add the carrots and kale in batches, stirring constantly. Cook for 2 minutes. Add the measured water, stock, lemon juice, potatoes, nutmeg and salt and pepper to taste. Bring to the boil, then reduce the heat, cover and simmer for 30–35 minutes or until all the vegetables are tender.

2 In a blender or food processor, blend the soup in batches, then transfer it to a clean saucepan. Add a little water if it is too thick.

3 Meanwhile, make the croûtons. Heat the oil in a large frying pan, add the garlic and cook over a moderate heat for 1 minute. Add the bread and cook, turning frequently, until golden brown. Remove with a slotted spoon and drain on kitchen paper. Remove and discard the garlic. Add the shredded kale and cook, stirring constantly, until crispy.

4 Reheat the soup gently. Serve in warm soup bowls, garnished with the croûtons and crispy kale.

25
PREP

45
COOK

8
SERVES

stylish

50 g (2 oz) **butter**

1 **onion**, chopped

2 **carrots**, sliced

500 g (1 lb) **kale**, stalks discarded

1.2 litres (2 pints) **water**

600 ml (1 pint) **Vegetable Stock** (see page 19)

1 tablespoon **lemon juice**

300 g (10 oz) **potatoes**, sliced

pinch of **grated nutmeg**

salt and **pepper**

2 **kale leaves**, thinly shredded, to garnish

GARLIC CROÛTONS:

6–8 tablespoons **olive oil**

3 **garlic cloves**, sliced

6–8 slices of white or brown **bread**, crusts removed, cut into 1 cm (½ inch) squares

Greens soup

20

PREP

75

COOK

6

SERVES

simple

500 g (1 lb) **kale**, stalks discarded

500 g (1 lb) **greens**, stalks discarded, roughly chopped

250 g (8 oz) **leeks**, sliced

1 teaspoon **caraway seeds**

3 **garlic cloves**, crushed

1 tablespoon **olive oil**

1.8 litres (3 pints) **water**

150 ml (¼ pint) **dry white wine**

125 g (4 oz) **ricotta cheese**

125 ml (4 fl oz) **crème fraîche**

125 ml (4 fl oz) **natural yogurt**

salt and **white pepper**

What a great way to eat your greens! This soup is full to bursting with healthy, tasty vegetables. The rather coarse texture gives it a rustic feel, and the colour is fantastic.

1 Mix the kale, greens, leeks, caraway seeds, garlic and oil in a large, heavy-based saucepan. Add the measured water, partially cover and bring to the boil. Reduce the heat and simmer for 45 minutes.

2 Drain the vegetables through a colander or sieve, reserving the liquid. In a blender or food processor, blend the vegetables until finely chopped but not puréed.

3 In a large, clean saucepan, combine 600 ml (1 pint) of the reserved liquid with the wine. Cook over a low heat for 3 minutes, then whisk in the ricotta cheese, crème fraîche and yogurt. Stir well and simmer for a further 3 minutes. Add the finely chopped vegetables. Stir in most of the remaining liquid to make a fairly thick soup.

4 Partially cover and simmer gently without boiling, stirring occasionally, for 20 minutes. Season to taste with salt and pepper. Serve immediately in warm soup bowls.

Parsley soup

10 PREP

In this soup recipe, parsley is used more as a vegetable than a herb. With its wonderful, fresh flavour, it's a shame to bring it out only for garnishes, and this soup proves it should be used more often.

55 COOK

1 Put the parsley and measured water in a saucepan and bring to the boil, then reduce the heat, cover and simmer for 30 minutes.

2 Rub the mixture through a sieve set over a large bowl. Discard the parsley remaining in the sieve.

4 SERVES

3 Melt the butter in a large, heavy-based saucepan, add the onion and cook over a moderate heat for 5 minutes or until softened. Add the parsley liquid and potatoes and bring to the boil, then reduce the heat, cover and simmer for about 15–20 minutes until the potatoes are tender.

herby

4 Add the nutmeg and salt and pepper to taste. Serve the soup in warm soup bowls, garnishing each portion with parsley leaves.

150 g (5 oz) **parsley**, plus extra leaves to garnish

600 ml (1 pint) **water**

25 g (1 oz) **butter**

1 **onion**, finely chopped

425 g (14 oz) **potatoes**, cut into 1 cm (½ inch) strips

¼ teaspoon **grated nutmeg**

salt and **white pepper**

50 g (2 oz) **butter**

1 **garlic clove**, crushed

1 **onion**, chopped

1 tablespoon mild **curry powder**

1.5 litres (2½ pints) **Vegetable Stock** (see page 19)

1 teaspoon chopped **marjoram**

1 **bay leaf**

500 g (1 lb) **green beans**, cut into 1 cm (½ inch) pieces

250–300 g (8–10 oz) **potatoes**, diced

salt

150 ml (¼ pint) **soured cream**, to garnish

15

PREP

55

COOK

6

SERVES

spicy

Curried green bean soup

Soured cream is the perfect garnish for spicy soups. It's important to add it to the bowls just before serving, because it will begin to melt into the soup immediately. The cool, almost tart, flavour will cut through the heat of the soup.

1 Melt the butter in a large, heavy-based saucepan, add the garlic and onion and cook over a moderate heat for 5 minutes or until softened but not browned. Stir in the curry powder and cook, stirring, for 2 minutes.

2 Pour in the stock and add the marjoram, bay leaf, beans and potatoes. Season to taste with salt. Bring to the boil, then reduce the heat, cover and simmer for 45 minutes or until the vegetables are tender. Remove and discard the bay leaf.

3 In a blender or food processor, blend the soup in batches until smooth, then return it to the saucepan. Reheat gently without boiling. Serve in warm soup bowls, garnishing each portion with a swirl of soured cream.

Cheddar cheese soup

10
PREP

15
COOK

Buy good-quality cheese to ensure that the soup has a rich flavour. Vintage varieties will obviously be stronger, so choose according to your personal taste.

6
SERVES

quick

1 Melt the butter in a large, heavy-based saucepan, add the onion and cook over a moderate heat for 5 minutes or until softened. Sprinkle in the flour and stir until well blended. Gradually add the warm stock, stirring constantly. Bring to the boil and cook, stirring constantly, until thickened.

2 Reduce the heat and stir in the milk, cheese and pepper. Season to taste with salt. Cook over a low heat, stirring constantly, until the cheese has melted and the soup begins to bubble. Serve immediately in warm soup bowls.

50 g (2 oz) **butter**

1 **onion**, finely grated

25 g (1 oz) **plain flour**

1 litre (1¾ pints) warm **Chicken Stock** (see page 17)

450 ml (¾ pint) **milk**

250 g (8 oz) **Cheddar cheese**, grated

½ teaspoon **white pepper**

salt

hearty

4 tablespoons extra virgin **olive oil**

1 large **onion**, chopped

50 g (2 oz) **chorizo sausage**, chopped

4 **garlic cloves**, crushed

2 tablespoons chopped **thyme**

1.2 litres (2 pints) **passata** (puréed tomatoes)

750 ml (1¼ pints) **Chicken Stock** (see page 17)

2 x 400 g (13 oz) cans **borlotti beans**, rinsed and drained

200 g (7 oz) **conchigliette** or other small pasta shapes

3 tablespoons chopped **basil**

salt and **pepper**

grated **Parmesan cheese**, to serve

15

PREP

35

COOK

6

SERVES

feast

Chunky chorizo, pasta and bean soup

This substantial winter soup is based on the Italian classic **pasta e fagioli** (pasta and beans). Pieces of fiery chorizo sausage add a lovely spiciness to the dish. The tiny pasta shapes used for soup are known as pastina, and there are dozens of different types to choose from.

1 Heat the oil in a large, heavy-based saucepan, add the onion, chorizo, garlic and thyme and cook over a moderate heat for 5 minutes. Add the passata, stock and beans. Season to taste with salt and pepper and bring to the boil, then reduce the heat, cover and simmer for 20 minutes.

2 Stir in the pasta and basil and simmer for a further 8–10 minutes or until the pasta is tender. Taste and adjust the seasoning if necessary. Ladle into warm bowls and serve topped with grated Parmesan.

Pumpkin soup with crusty cheese topping

If you prefer to make croûtons, grill the baguette slices on one side, then turn them over, top with the cheese and replace under the grill until the cheese begins to melt. They can be used to garnish many different soups.

25

PREP

60

COOK

4

SERVES

rich

1 Heat the oil in a large, heavy-based saucepan, add the onion and garlic and cook over a moderate heat for 5 minutes or until softened. Add the celery and pumpkin and cook for 10–15 minutes. Stir in the stock and nutmeg. Tie the bay leaf and parsley stalks together with string, add to the pan and bring to the boil. Reduce the heat and simmer for about 30 minutes until the vegetables are tender. Remove and discard the herbs.

2 In a blender or food processor, blend the soup in batches until smooth, then return it to the pan. Bring to the boil and season with salt and pepper. Stir in the cream and parsley and reheat gently without boiling.

3 Meanwhile, put the bread slices for the garnish on a baking sheet. Toast under a pre-heated hot grill until golden on both sides.

4 Pour the soup into 4 deep ovenproof bowls. Arrange 2 toast slices, overlapping, on each. Sprinkle with the cheese. Put on the baking sheet. Cook under the grill until the cheese is browned and bubbling. Serve immediately.

1½ tablespoons **olive oil**

1 large **onion**, finely chopped

3 **garlic cloves**, crushed

2 **celery sticks**, chopped

750 g (1½ lb) **pumpkin** flesh, roughly chopped

900 ml (1½ pints) **Vegetable Stock** (see page 19)

pinch of **grated nutmeg**

1 **bay leaf**

few **parsley** stalks

75 ml (3 fl oz) **single cream**

1–2 tablespoons finely chopped **parsley**

salt and **pepper**

TO GARNISH:

1 small **baguette**, cut into 8 slices

50 g (2 oz) **Gruyère cheese**, grated

6–8 **garlic cloves**, unpeeled

3 tablespoons **olive oil**

1 large **onion**, chopped

2 **celery sticks**, chopped

1 **leek**, chopped

6 **allspice berries**, crushed

1 sprig of **thyme**

1 **bay leaf**

2 **tomatoes**, skinned and chopped

50 g (2 oz) **peanut butter**

750 g (1½ lb) **pumpkin**, peeled and cubed

1.5 litres (2½ pints) **Vegetable Stock** (see page 19)

salt and **pepper**

TO SERVE:

200 ml (7 fl oz) **soured cream** or **crème fraîche**

breadsticks (optional)

20

PREP

60

COOK

4

SERVES

tasty

Pumpkin and peanut butter soup

This unusual recipe includes peanut butter, which adds a creamy, nutty contrast to the pumpkin. Allspice, thyme and bay round off the soup.

1 Put the garlic cloves in a small roasting tin and toss with 1 tablespoon of the oil. Roast in a preheated oven, 180°C (350°F), Gas Mark 4, for 15–20 minutes until softened. Leave until cool enough to handle, then pop the cloves out of their skins and reserve.

2 Heat the remaining oil in a large, heavy-based saucepan, add the onion, celery and leek and cook over a moderate heat for 8–10 minutes or until softened. Add the roasted garlic and all the remaining ingredients and bring to the boil. Reduce the heat and simmer, uncovered, for 20–30 minutes or until the vegetables are tender.

3 In a blender or food processor, blend the soup in batches until smooth. Strain through a sieve into the pan. Reheat thoroughly. Serve the soup in warm soup bowls, topped with a spoonful of soured cream or crème fraîche and accompanied by breadsticks for dunking, if liked.

Chunky carrot and lentil soup

10

PREP

35

COOK

This nutritious soup is substantial enough for a main course if you serve it with some good crusty bread. A zesty, spiced butter, stirred in at the table, adds a lively flavour.

1 Make the spiced butter, if serving. Put all the ingredients in a bowl and beat together until combined. Transfer to a small serving dish, cover and chill until ready to serve.

2 Heat the oil in a large, heavy-based saucepan, add the onion and celery and cook over a moderate heat for 5 minutes or until softened. Add the carrots and garlic and cook, stirring, for 3 minutes. Add the lentils and stock and bring just to the boil. Reduce the heat, cover and simmer for 20–25 minutes until the vegetables are tender and the soup is pulpy. Season to taste with salt and pepper.

3 Ladle the soup into warm bowls and serve the spiced butter (if using) at the table, so that diners can stir in as much as they like.

4

SERVES

spicy

2 tablespoons **vegetable oil**

1 large **onion**, chopped

2 **celery sticks**, sliced

500 g (1 lb) **carrots**, sliced

1 **garlic clove**, crushed

150 g (5 oz) **split red lentils**, washed and drained

1.4 litres (2¼ pints) **Vegetable Stock** (see page 19)

salt and **pepper**

SPICED BUTTER (OPTIONAL):

40 g (1½ oz) **lightly salted butter**, softened

2 **spring onions**, finely chopped

¼ teaspoon dried **chilli flakes**

1 teaspoon **cumin seeds**, lightly crushed

finely grated rind of 1 **lemon**

small handful of fresh **coriander**, chopped

several sprigs of **mint**, chopped

1 tablespoon **olive oil**

1 **onion**, chopped

2 **carrots**, diced

1 **red pepper**, cored, deseeded and diced

2 **garlic cloves**, chopped (optional)

1 small **red chilli**, deseeded and chopped

1 teaspoon **cumin seeds**

400 g (13 oz) can **red kidney beans**, drained and rinsed

500 g (1 lb) carton **creamed tomatoes**

600 ml (1 pint) **Vegetable Stock** (see page 19)

1 tablespoon **soft dark brown sugar**

salt and **pepper**

TO GARNISH:

Greek yogurt

paprika

cumin seeds

15

PREP

40

COOK

4

SERVES

thick

Chunky chilli bean and carrot soup

This warming soup has just a hint of chilli. It is made with ingredients that you are likely to have in store, so it makes a good standby for days when you haven't time to shop. If you don't have a red pepper, you could add an extra carrot.

1 Heat the oil in a large, heavy-based saucepan, add the onion and cook over a moderate heat for 5 minutes or until softened. Add the carrots, red pepper and garlic (if using) and cook, stirring, for 3 minutes or until softened. Stir in the chilli and cumin and cook, stirring, for 1 minute.

2 Add the beans, creamed tomatoes, stock and sugar and season to taste with salt and pepper. Bring to the boil, then reduce the heat, cover and simmer for 30 minutes or until reduced and thickened.

3 Ladle the soup into bowls and serve topped with a spoonful of yogurt and a sprinkling of paprika and cumin seeds.

Carrot soup with orange and ginger

Carrots team well with garlic and ginger in this tasty soup, and the fresh orange juice provides an unexpected flavour as well as intensifying the colour. This soup can be served lukewarm or cold if you prefer.

10

PREP

20

COOK

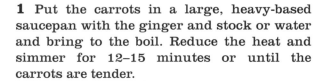

6

SERVES

fresh

750 g (1½ lb) **carrots**, roughly chopped

5 cm (2 inch) piece of fresh **root ginger**, peeled and finely chopped

900 ml (1½ pints) **Vegetable Stock** (see page 19) or **water**

2 tablespoons chopped **parsley**

150 ml (¼ pint) **orange juice**

salt and **pepper**

buttermilk or **thick natural yogurt**, to serve

1 Put the carrots in a large, heavy-based saucepan with the ginger and stock or water and bring to the boil. Reduce the heat and simmer for 12–15 minutes or until the carrots are tender.

2 In a blender or food processor, blend the soup with the parsley and orange juice in batches until smooth, then return to the pan.

3 Season to taste with salt and pepper. Reheat gently, then serve the soup in warm soup bowls with a little buttermilk or yogurt swirled on top.

2 tablespoons **olive oil**

1 large **onion**, chopped

1–2 **garlic cloves**, crushed

1 tablespoon finely grated fresh **root ginger**

375 g (12 oz) **carrots**, sliced

900 ml (1½ pints) **Vegetable Stock** (see page 19)

2 tablespoons **lime juice** or **lemon juice**

salt and **pepper**

TO SERVE:

soured cream

2 **spring onions**, finely chopped

15
PREP

30
COOK

4
SERVES

tasty

Carrot and ginger soup

Carrots have a naturally sweet flavour that works well with ginger. This is a good winter soup – ginger is believed to have many health benefits, which include helping to fight off colds and flu.

1 Heat the oil in a large, heavy-based saucepan, add the onion, garlic and ginger and cook over a moderate heat for 5 minutes or until softened.

2 Add the carrots and stock and bring to the boil. Reduce the heat and simmer for 15–20 minutes or until the carrots are tender.

3 In a blender or food processor, blend the soup with the lime or lemon juice in batches until smooth. Strain through a sieve into the pan. Reheat gently, then serve the soup in warm soup bowls with a spoonful of soured cream and sprinkled with finely chopped spring onions.

Tomato chowder

This is a fantastic stand-by recipe because it can be made from storecupboard ingredients. It's also very quick to prepare, so there are no excuses for not making your own soup!

1 Mix together all the ingredients except the cheese in a large, heavy-based saucepan. Bring slowly to the boil, stirring constantly, then reduce the heat and simmer, uncovered, for 3 minutes.

2 Ladle the soup into warm ovenproof bowls and sprinkle with the cheese. Put on a baking sheet and cook under a preheated hot grill for 3–5 minutes or until the cheese is browned and bubbling. Serve immediately.

5

PREP

12

COOK

4

SERVES

quick

300 g (10 oz) can **condensed tomato soup**

400 g (13 oz) can **tomatoes**, sieved

325 g (11 oz) can **sweetcorn kernels**, drained

1 tablespoon **Worcestershire sauce**

3–6 drops of **Tabasco sauce**

1 teaspoon chopped **oregano**

½ teaspoon **caster sugar**

125 g (4 oz) **Cheddar cheese**, grated

1 tablespoon **olive oil**

1 **onion**, finely chopped

400 g (13 oz) can **plum tomatoes**

½ teaspoon **caster sugar**

300 ml (½ pint) **Chicken Stock** (see page 17)

2 tablespoons **tomato purée**

50 g (2 oz) small **pasta shapes**

75 g (3 oz) frozen **broad beans**

40 g (1½ oz) **Cheddar cheese** or **Gruyère cheese**, crumbled

salt and **pepper**

5

PREP

20

COOK

2

SERVES

easy

Tomato, broad bean and pasta soup

Canned tomatoes and tiny soup pasta are the main ingredients in this comforting, minestrone-style soup. Served topped with crumbled cheese, it is delicious accompanied by lightly toasted grainy bread.

1 Heat the oil in a large, heavy-based saucepan, add the onion and cook over a moderate heat for 5 minutes or until softened. Add the tomatoes, sugar, stock and tomato purée and bring to the boil. Reduce the heat, cover and simmer for 5 minutes. Add the pasta, cover and cook for 5 minutes or until the pasta is tender.

2 Stir in the beans and salt and pepper to taste. Simmer for a further 2 minutes or until the beans are tender. Ladle into warm soup bowls and serve sprinkled with the cheese.

Roasted tomato and chilli soup

The combination of tomato and chilli is used in many dishes, from curries to pasta sauces, and with good reason. The black olives add a salty contrast to the sweet tomatoes and hot chillies, while lime adds the sour element, making this a perfect dish for the taste buds.

20 PREP

70 COOK

4 SERVES

hot

1 Lightly grease a baking sheet with a little of the oil, lay the tomatoes on top, cut side up, and sprinkle with 4 tablespoons of the oil, the salt and sugar. Add the chilli and roast in a preheated oven, 180°C (350°F), Gas Mark 4, for 45–50 minutes. Remove the chilli after 20 minutes. Leave to cool, then peel off the skin, deseed and chop the flesh roughly.

2 Meanwhile, make the olive cream. Fold the olives into the crème fraîche.

3 Heat the remaining oil in a large, heavy-based saucepan, add the onion and cook over a moderate heat until golden. Add the garlic and cook, stirring, for 2 minutes. Add the roasted tomatoes, the reserved juice and seeds, chilli and measured water. Bring to the boil. Reduce the heat and simmer for 10–12 minutes. Season to taste with salt and pepper.

4 In a blender or food processor, blend the soup in batches until smooth. Strain through a fine sieve into the pan. Add lime juice and reheat. Serve in warm soup bowls with a spoonful of the olive cream in each portion.

1.5 kg (3 lb) ripe **tomatoes**, preferably plum, deseeded and juice and seeds reserved

6 tablespoons extra virgin **olive oil**

1½ teaspoons **sea salt**

1 tablespoon **caster sugar**

1 large **red chilli**

1 **onion**, chopped

1 **garlic clove**, crushed

600 ml (1 pint) **water**

2–4 tablespoons **lime juice**

salt and **pepper**

OLIVE CREAM:

50 g (2 oz) pitted **black olives**, finely chopped

50 g (2 oz) **crème fraîche**

1 tablespoon **sunflower** oil

1 **onion**, finely chopped

15 g (½ oz) **butter**

2 **carrots**, about 250 g (8 oz) in total, diced

1 **potato**, about 250 g (8 oz), diced

1 **parsnip**, about 250 g (8 oz), diced

½ teaspoon **ground turmeric**

3 teaspoons mild **curry paste**

1.2 litres (2 pints) **Vegetable Stock** (see page 19)

75 g (3 oz) **red lentils**, washed and drained

salt and **pepper**

chopped **parsley**, to garnish

15

PREP

55

COOK

4

SERVES

filling

Vegetable and lentil hotpot

This budget-priced soup is a good way to use up the oddments from the vegetable rack and is tasty without being too spicy. It would make a great low-calorie lunch.

1 Heat the oil in a large, heavy-based saucepan, add the onion and cook over a moderate heat for 5 minutes or until softened. Add the butter and the diced vegetables and cook, stirring frequently, for 5 minutes.

2 Stir in the turmeric and curry paste and cook, stirring, for 1 minute. Add the stock and lentils, then season to taste with salt and pepper. Bring to the boil, then reduce the heat, cover and simmer for 40 minutes or until the lentils are tender.

3 Ladle into warm soup bowls and serve sprinkled with chopped parsley.

Curried lentil soup

Unlike dried pulses, red, Puy and continental lentils do not need soaking before use. If you don't have one of the vegetables listed, replace it with something that you do have, such as a little diced swede, some butternut squash, a courgette or some tomatoes.

1 Heat the oil in large, heavy-based saucepan, add the onion and cook over a moderate heat for 5 minutes or until softened. Add the garlic, potato, carrot, celery and curry paste and cook, stirring occasionally, for 5 minutes.

2 Add the lentils, tomatoes, stock and salt and pepper to taste. Bring to the boil, then reduce the heat, cover and simmer for 30 minutes or until the lentils are tender.

3 Ladle into warm soup bowls and serve sprinkled with chopped coriander.

15

PREP

45

COOK

4

SERVES

spicy

1 tablespoon **vegetable oil**

1 small **onion**, finely chopped

1 **garlic clove**, crushed

1 small **potato**, finely diced

1 **carrot**, finely diced

2 **celery sticks**, finely chopped

1 tablespoon mild **curry paste**

50 g (2 oz) **red lentils**, washed and drained

200 g (7 oz) can chopped **tomatoes**

600 ml (1 pint) **Chicken Stock** (see page 17)

salt and **pepper**

chopped fresh **coriander**, to garnish

1 tablespoon **vegetable oil**

1 large **onion**, chopped

2 **garlic cloves**, chopped

1 small **green chilli**, deseeded and finely chopped (optional)

250 g (8 oz) **red lentils**, washed and drained

1 **bay leaf**

3 **celery sticks**, thinly sliced

3 **carrots**, thinly sliced

1 **leek**, thinly sliced

1.5 litres (2½ pints) **Vegetable Stock** (see page 19)

400 g (13 oz) can chopped **tomatoes**

2 tablespoons **tomato purée**

½ teaspoon **ground turmeric**

½ teaspoon **ground ginger**

1 tablespoon chopped fresh **coriander**

pepper

natural yogurt, to garnish

20 PREP

50 COOK

4 SERVES

hot

Spicy lentil and tomato soup

The lentils will break down when they are cooked, thickening the soup as well as adding plenty of flavour. The soup will keep in the refrigerator for up to three days, or you could freeze individual portions.

1 Heat the oil in a large, heavy-based saucepan, add the onion, garlic and chilli (if using) and cook over a moderate heat for 5 minutes or until softened. Add the lentils, bay leaf, celery, carrots, leek and stock. Cover and bring to the boil, then reduce the heat and simmer for 30–40 minutes until the lentils are tender. Remove and discard the bay leaf.

2 Stir in the tomatoes, tomato purée, turmeric, ginger and coriander. Season to taste with pepper.

3 In a blender or food processor, blend the soup in batches until smooth, adding more stock or water if necessary then return it to the pan. Reheat gently. Ladle the soup into warm soup bowls and serve, each portion garnished with a swirl of yogurt.

Armenian onion and lentil soup

This soup is simmered for over an hour to allow the barley and lentils to cook until tender and absorb the flavour of the onion, herbs and spices.

15

PREP

105

COOK

8

SERVES

tasty

1 Wash the barley in a colander under cold running water. Drain well and tip into a large, heavy-based saucepan. Pour in the measured water. Bring to the boil, then reduce the heat, partially cover and simmer, stirring occasionally, for 25–30 minutes or until all the water is absorbed.

2 Add the stock, onions, lentils, tarragon, paprika, cayenne pepper, sugar and wine. Bring to the boil. Reduce the heat, partially cover and simmer for about 1¼ hours. Add a little more water if the soup is too thick. Season to taste with salt and pepper.

3 Meanwhile, melt the butter for the garnish in a small frying pan. Add the onion and cook over a moderate heat for 5 minutes or until softened and golden.

4 Ladle the soup into warm soup bowls and serve garnished with the chopped onion.

25 g (1 oz) **pearl barley**

150 ml (¼ pint) **water**

1.8 litres (3 pints) **Beef Stock** (see page 18)

500 g (1 lb) **onions**, thinly sliced

150 g (5 oz) **green lentils**, washed and drained

1 teaspoon **dried tarragon**

2 teaspoons **paprika**

pinch of **cayenne pepper**

¼ teaspoon **caster sugar**

3 tablespoons **dry white wine**

salt and **pepper**

TO GARNISH:

25 g (1 oz) **butter**

3 tablespoons finely chopped mild **onion**

1.5 kg (3 lb) free-range **chicken**

2–4 tablespoons **olive oil**

1 **onion**, chopped

4 **garlic cloves**, crushed

1 teaspoon grated fresh **root ginger**

2 teaspoons **paprika**

¼ teaspoon **saffron threads**

2 x 400 g (13 oz) cans chopped **tomatoes**

900 ml (1½ pints) **water**

125 g (4 oz) cooked **chickpeas** (from a can)

50 g (2 oz) **red lentils**, washed and drained

50 g (2 oz) **basmati rice**

4 tablespoons **lemon juice**

2 tablespoons chopped **parsley**

2 tablespoons chopped fresh **coriander**

1–2 tablespoons **harissa paste** (optional)

salt and **pepper**

grilled **pitta bread**, to serve

20

PREP

65

COOK

8

SERVES

exotic

Harira

Harira is eaten throughout North Africa and the Middle East. Made with lamb or chicken and flavoured with lemon and tomatoes, the soup would traditionally have been thickened with yeast or flour. It tastes even better the next day when it thickens naturally, as the liquid is absorbed by the rice and lentils.

1 Joint the chicken into 8 pieces. Heat 2 tablespoons oil in a saucepan, add the chicken pieces and cook until browned on all sides. Remove with a slotted spoon.

2 Add more oil to the pan if necessary. Add the onion, garlic and ginger and cook over a moderate heat for 10 minutes or until golden. Return the chicken to the pan and add all the remaining ingredients, except the herbs and harissa, with salt and pepper to taste. Cover and simmer gently for 45 minutes.

3 Remove the chicken pieces and leave to cool slightly, then gently pull the flesh away from the bones. Return the meat to the soup. Leave the soup to cool completely, then cover and chill overnight.

4 Reheat the soup, then stir in the herbs and harissa (if using). Serve in warm soup bowls with grilled pitta bread.

Bean soup with garlic and chilli oil

This is a substantial soup from Tuscany. To give it a sophisticated touch, sliced garlic is fried in chilli-flavoured olive oil, then poured over the soup at the last moment. The beans may take less time to cook, depending on their freshness, so test after 40 minutes.

35*
PREP

80
COOK

6
SERVES

stylish

250 g (8 oz) dried **white beans**, such as haricot or cannellini, soaked overnight in cold water

Chicken Stock (see page 17) or **water**

handful of **sage** leaves

4 **garlic cloves**, 2 finely chopped, 2 thinly sliced

150 ml (¼ pint) **olive oil**

2 tablespoons chopped **sage** or **rosemary**

good pinch of dried **chilli flakes**

salt and **pepper**

1 Drain the beans and put in a flameproof casserole. Cover with the stock or cold water to come 5 cm (2 inches) above the beans. Push in the sage leaves. Bring to the boil, then cover tightly and bake in a preheated oven, 160°C (325°F), Gas Mark 3, for about 1 hour or until tender. Leave in the cooking liquid.

2 In a blender or food processor, blend half of the beans with the sage and all the liquid until smooth. Return to the casserole with the remaining beans. Add more water or stock if the soup is too thick.

3 Heat half of the oil in a nonstick frying pan, add the chopped garlic and cook over a moderate heat until golden. Add the herbs and cook for 30 seconds. Stir into the soup and bring to the boil. Reduce the heat and simmer gently for 10 minutes. Season to taste with salt and pepper. Pour into a warm tureen.

4 Cook the sliced garlic in the remaining oil until golden, then stir in the chilli flakes. Dip the base of the pan into cold water to stop the garlic cooking, then spoon over the soup.

* Plus overnight soaking

3 tablespoons **olive oil**

2 **garlic cloves**, crushed

1 small **red pepper**, cored, deseeded and chopped

1 **onion**, finely chopped

250 g (8 oz) **tomatoes**, finely chopped

1 teaspoon finely chopped **thyme**

125 g (4 oz) **haricot beans**, soaked overnight in cold water, rinsed and drained

600 ml (1 pint) **water**

600 ml (1 pint) **Vegetable Stock** (see page 19)

2 tablespoons finely chopped **parsley**

salt and **pepper**

15 *

PREP

75

COOK

6

SERVES

posh

White bean soup Provençal

Haricot beans are one of the staples of Mediterranean cuisine, and they make good, thick soups that are ideal for winter evenings. You can use any white bean, such as cannellini, if you have them in store, but adjust the cooking time – the older they are, the longer they take.

1 Heat the oil in a large, heavy-based saucepan, add the garlic, red pepper and onion and cook over a moderate heat for 5 minutes or until softened.

2 Add the tomatoes and thyme and cook for 1 minute. Add the beans and pour in the measured water and stock. Bring to the boil, then reduce the heat, cover and simmer for 1 hour.

3 Add the parsley and season to taste with salt and pepper. Serve immediately in warm soup bowls.

* Plus overnight soaking

Bean and cabbage soup

Earthy dried beans team perfectly with spicy chorizo and cabbage in this satisfying soup, which makes a complete meal in itself served with hunks of fresh crusty bread.

20* PREP

110 COOK

4 SERVES

filling

1 Put the beans in a large, heavy-based saucepan with 125 g (4 oz) chorizo in a piece, the rosemary, bouquet garni and measured water. Bring to the boil and boil rapidly for 10 minutes, then reduce the heat, cover and simmer gently for 1–1½ hours or until the beans are tender.

2 Meanwhile, heat the oil in a nonstick frying pan, add the onion, garlic, red pepper and cayenne pepper and cook over a moderate heat for 5 minutes. Dice the remaining chorizo, add to the pan and cook for a further 5 minutes.

3 Stir the onion mixture into the cooked beans with the cabbage. Season to taste with salt and pepper, bring to the boil and cook for 20 minutes. Add the parsley and taste and adjust the seasoning if necessary. Spoon into warm bowls. Drizzle with olive oil and serve immediately with crusty bread.

175 g (6 oz) dried **broad beans**, soaked overnight in cold water, rinsed and drained

250 g (8 oz) **chorizo sausage**

2 sprigs of **rosemary**

1 **bouquet garni**

1.8 litres (3 pints) cold **water**

2 tablespoons **olive oil**

1 **onion**, chopped

2 **garlic cloves**, crushed

1 small **red pepper**, cored, deseeded and chopped

pinch of **cayenne pepper**

250 g (8 oz) **Savoy cabbage**, shredded

1 tablespoon chopped **parsley**

salt and **pepper**

TO SERVE:

olive oil

crusty **bread**

* Plus overnight soaking

WHITE BEAN SOUP:

250 g (8 oz) dried **haricot beans** or **cannellini beans**, soaked overnight in cold water, drained and rinsed

900 ml (1½ pints) **water**

salt and **pepper**

ROCKET SOUP:

25 g (1 oz) **butter**

1 **onion**, chopped

2 **potatoes**, about 250 g (8 oz) in total, cut into 1.5 cm (¾ inch) dice

200 g (7 oz) **rocket**, roughly chopped

300 ml (½ pint) **Vegetable Stock** (see page 19)

300 ml (½ pint) **milk**

100 ml (3½ fl oz) **double cream**

45*

PREP

65

COOK

4

SERVES

party

* Plus overnight soaking

Rocket and white bean twin soup

This recipe takes a little preparation and a steady hand, but it's well worth the effort. The stark contrast in colours when the two soups are sitting in the bowls really is stunning – save it for special occasions.

1 Make the white bean soup. Put the beans in a saucepan and cover with the measured water. Bring to the boil, then reduce the heat and simmer for 45–60 minutes or until tender. In a blender or food processor, blend the beans and their liquid in batches. Press through a fine sieve into the pan. Season to taste with salt and pepper.

2 Meanwhile, make the rocket soup. Melt the butter in a large, heavy-based saucepan, add the onion and cook over a moderate heat for 5 minutes or until softened. Add the potatoes, cover and cook for 5 minutes. Add the rocket, cover and cook for 3–4 minutes or until just wilted. Add the stock, milk and salt and pepper to taste, then simmer for 10 minutes until the potatoes are tender. In a blender or food processor, blend in batches until smooth. Strain through a sieve into a clean pan.

3 Reheat the 2 soups separately. Add the cream to the rocket soup and heat through. Add more stock or water to the bean soup to make the same consistency. Using 2 ladles, pour the 2 soups simultaneously into bowls.

Spanish chickpea soup

15*

PREP

145

COOK

8

SERVES

thick

Known as **garbanzo** in Spain, **ceci** in Italy and **chana dal** in India, the chickpea is a staple part of the Middle Eastern diet and is used in many European dishes, particularly stews and thick soups like this one.

1 Drain the chickpeas, rinse under cold running water and drain again. Put the bacon joint in a large, deep saucepan and cover with cold water. Bring the water briefly to the boil, then drain, discarding the water.

2 Put the bacon joint in a large, heavy-based clean saucepan. Add the chickpeas, studded onion, garlic, bay leaf, thyme, marjoram, parsley and measured water. Bring to the boil, then reduce the heat, partially cover and simmer for 1½ hours. Remove and discard the onion and herbs. Remove the hock, transfer to a board and cut into small pieces. Set aside.

3 Add the stock, potatoes and cabbage to the pan and simmer for a further 30 minutes. Add the reserved hock pieces to the soup and cook for a further 10 minutes. Season to taste with salt and pepper. Serve the soup in warm soup bowls.

150 g (5 oz) dried **chickpeas**, soaked for 48 hours in cold water or 12 hours in boiling water

500–750 g (1–1½ lb) boneless **smoked bacon hock joint**

1 **onion**, studded with 4 **cloves**

2 **garlic cloves**, crushed

1 **bay leaf**

1 sprig of **thyme**

1 sprig of **marjoram**

1 sprig of **parsley**

1.8 litres (3 pints) **water**

1.8 litres (3 pints) **Chicken Stock** (see page 17)

300–375 g (10–12 oz) **potatoes**, cut into 1 cm (½ inch) cubes

300 g (10 oz) **Savoy cabbage**, shredded

salt and **pepper**

* Plus 12–48 hours soaking

50 g (2 oz) **butter**

1 **onion**, chopped

1 **garlic clove**, crushed

50 g (2 oz) **red lentils**, washed and drained

50 g (2 oz) **white long-grain rice**

1.8 litres (3 pints) **Vegetable Stock** (see page 19)

1 bunch of **watercress**, stalks discarded, roughly chopped

425 g (14 oz) can **chickpeas**, drained and rinsed

salt and **pepper**

10

PREP

35

COOK

4

SERVES

easy

Chickpea and watercress soup

This hearty soup is ideal for vegetarians (non-vegetarians could use chicken stock) because it contains protein carbohydrates and plenty of vitamins – a meal in a bowl. Serve with wholemeal bread.

1 Melt the butter in a large, heavy-based saucepan, add the onion and garlic and cook for 5 minutes or until the onion is softened.

2 Add the lentils and rice and stir well. Pour in the stock and bring to the boil, then reduce the heat, cover and simmer for 15–18 minutes or until the lentils and rice are tender.

3 Add the watercress and chickpeas. Simmer the soup for a further 8–10 minutes. Season to taste with salt and pepper and serve in warm soup bowls.

Minestrone soup

Minestrone improves when it is made in advance and reheated. Cover and store in the refrigerator so that the flavours can blend.

20
PREP

25
COOK

4
SERVES

classic

1 Heat the oil in a large, heavy-based saucepan, add the onion, garlic, celery, leek and carrot and cook over a moderate heat for 3 minutes.

2 Stir in the tomatoes, stock, courgette, cabbage, bay leaf and beans. Bring to the boil, then reduce the heat and simmer gently for 10 minutes.

3 Add the spaghetti and season to taste with salt and pepper, then stir well and simmer, stirring frequently, for a further 8 minutes.

4 Add the parsley and stir well. Ladle into warm soup bowls, scatter with the grated Parmesan and serve with bruschetta.

2 tablespoons **olive oil**

1 **onion**, diced

1 **garlic clove**, crushed

2 **celery sticks**, chopped

1 **leek**, thinly sliced

1 **carrot**, chopped

400 g (13 oz) can chopped **tomatoes**

600 ml (1 pint) **Vegetable Stock** (see page 19)

1 **courgette**, diced

½ small **cabbage**, shredded

1 **bay leaf**

75 g (3 oz) can **haricot beans**, rinsed and drained

75 g (3 oz) **spaghetti**, broken into small pieces

1 tablespoon chopped **flat leaf parsley**

salt and **pepper**

TO SERVE:

50 g (2 oz) **Parmesan cheese**, grated

bruschetta

50 g (2 oz) dried **haricot beans**, soaked overnight in cold water

3 tablespoons **olive oil**

2 **garlic cloves**, crushed

1 **celery stick**, chopped

2 **leeks**, sliced

3 **tomatoes**, chopped

3 tablespoons chopped **flat leaf parsley**

2 tablespoons chopped **basil**

125 g (4 oz) **green beans**, cut into 2.5 cm (1 inch) pieces

125 g (4 oz) **asparagus**, cut into 2.5 cm (1 inch) pieces

1 litre (1¾ pints) boiling **Vegetable Stock** (see page 19) or **water**

75 g (3 oz) **white long-grain rice**

175 g (6 oz) **spinach**

150 g (5 oz) frozen **broad beans**, skinned

125 g (4 oz) frozen **peas**

salt and **pepper**

50 g (2 oz) **Parmesan cheese**, grated, to serve

30*

PREP

110

COOK

6

SERVES

simple

* Plus overnight soaking

Minestrone verde

An Italian classic that is a real meal in a bowl. Hearty green vegetables, beans, rice and plenty of fresh herbs make a soup that's so substantial you won't need bread as well.

1 Drain the haricot beans, rinse under cold running water and drain again. Put in a saucepan and cover with cold water. Bring to the boil, then reduce the heat and simmer for 45–60 minutes or until tender. Remove from the heat and leave in the cooking liquid.

2 Heat the oil in a large, heavy-based saucepan, add the garlic, celery and leeks and cook over a moderate heat for 5–10 minutes or until softened. Add the tomatoes with half of the herbs and salt and pepper to taste, then simmer for 12–15 minutes until the tomatoes become pulpy.

3 Add the green beans and asparagus. Cook for 1–2 minutes, then add the stock or water. Bring to the boil and boil rapidly for 10 minutes. Add the rice, cooked haricot beans and their liquid, spinach, broad beans and peas and cook for 10 minutes. Taste and adjust the seasoning if necessary. Ladle the soup into warm soup bowls and serve the Parmesan separately.

Parsnip and orange soup

15

PREP

45

COOK

6

SERVES

fresh

The humble, inexpensive parsnip can be transformed into a number of delicious soups. The addition of fresh orange imparts a distinctive flavour and colour.

1 Melt the butter in a large, heavy-based saucepan and add the parsnips, onion, potato and nutmeg (if using). Cover and cook over a low to moderate heat, stirring occasionally, for 10 minutes.

2 Add the orange juice, orange rind strips and stock. Bring to the boil, then reduce the heat, cover and simmer for 30 minutes. Remove and discard the orange rind strips.

3 In a blender or food processor, blend the soup in batches until smooth, then transfer it to a clean saucepan. Add a little water if the soup is too thick.

4 Mix the lemon juice with the cream in a jug and stir into the soup. Reheat gently without boiling. Season to taste with salt and pepper. Ladle into warm soup bowls and serve immediately, garnishing each portion with an orange segment.

125 g (4 oz) **butter**

1.5 kg (3 lb) **parsnips**, scrubbed and roughly chopped

1 **onion**, chopped

1 **potato**, chopped

grated nutmeg (optional)

150 ml (¼ pint) freshly squeezed **orange juice**

pared **rind** of 1 **orange**, cut into wide strips

1.8 litres (3 pints) **Chicken Stock** (see page 17)

1 teaspoon **lemon juice**

125 ml (4 fl oz) **double cream**

salt and **white pepper**

6–8 **orange segments**, to garnish

3 tablespoons extra virgin **olive oil**

3 large **red onions**, sliced

1 **fennel bulb**, trimmed and thinly sliced

1 **garlic clove**, crushed

2 tablespoons **red wine vinegar**

1 **bay leaf**

2 sprigs of **thyme**

½ teaspoon **dried pink peppercorns**, crushed

150 ml (¼ pint) **red wine**

600 ml (1 pint) **Chicken Stock** (see page 17)

salt and **pepper**

CROÛTONS:

8 slices of **French bread**

4 thin slices from a **goats' cheese** log, cut in half

10

PREP

55

COOK

4

SERVES

posh

Red onion soup with goats' cheese

Make sure you choose a soft goats' cheese for the croûtons. The cheese needs to soften and begin to melt and bubble; hard varieties won't do this successfully. Also, pick a fairly decent red wine – using cheap plonk for cooking is a false economy.

1 Heat the oil in a large, heavy-based saucepan, add the onions, fennel and garlic and cook over a moderate heat for 5 minutes or until softened. Sprinkle with a little salt, then reduce the heat, cover and cook for 30–35 minutes. Increase the heat, add the vinegar and boil for 1–2 minutes until the liquid is reduced by half.

2 Add the bay leaf, thyme, peppercorns, wine and stock. Bring to the boil, then reduce the heat and simmer for 10–15 minutes. Remove the thyme and bay leaf and taste and adjust the seasoning if necessary.

3 Meanwhile, make the croûtons. Put the bread slices under a preheated hot grill and toast lightly on one side. Turn the slices over and top each one with a slice of goats' cheese. Return to the grill and toast until the cheese is bubbling and browned. Serve immediately with the hot soup in warm bowls.

Courgette and mint soup

20
PREP

25
COOK

Courgette, mint and lemon make a delicately flavoured soup, which is thickened with egg yolks and finished with a generous helping of double cream.

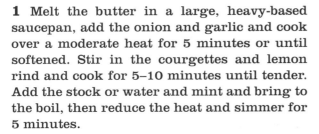

4
SERVES

herby

1 Melt the butter in a large, heavy-based saucepan, add the onion and garlic and cook over a moderate heat for 5 minutes or until softened. Stir in the courgettes and lemon rind and cook for 5–10 minutes until tender. Add the stock or water and mint and bring to the boil, then reduce the heat and simmer for 5 minutes.

2 In a blender or food processor, blend the soup in batches until smooth. Strain through a sieve into the pan. The soup can be prepared ahead up to this point.

3 Just before serving, reheat the soup to just below boiling point. In a small bowl, mix the egg yolks and cream and whisk in a ladleful of the hot soup. Whisk the mixture into the soup and heat gently without boiling. Season to taste with salt and pepper and serve immediately in warm soup bowls.

50 g (2 oz) **butter**

1 small **onion**, chopped

1–2 **garlic cloves**, crushed

750 g (1½ lb) **courgettes**, diced

finely grated rind of 1 **lemon**

600 ml (1 pint) **Chicken Stock** (see page 17) or **water**

2–3 tablespoons chopped **mint**

2 **egg yolks**

100 ml (3½ fl oz) **double cream**

salt and **pepper**

3 teaspoons **cumin seeds**

3 tablespoons **olive oil**

1 **onion**, chopped

1 **garlic clove**, crushed

4 **red peppers**, roasted, skinned, deseeded (see page 90) and diced

1 litre (1¾ pints) **Chicken Stock** (see page 17)

salt and **pepper**

CORIANDER OIL:

75 g (3 oz) fresh **coriander**, including stalks

125 ml (4 fl oz) extra virgin **olive oil**

45

PREP

55

COOK

4

SERVES

spicy

Roasted red pepper and cumin soup

Roasted peppers have a sweet, smoky flavour and they need few other ingredients. Here, they are combined with just a few herbs and spices, as well as fresh chicken stock. Use the coriander oil within 1 week of making.

1 Make the coriander oil. Blanch the coriander for 5–10 seconds in a saucepan of boiling water. Drain and refresh in cold water. Drain well and squeeze out all the liquid in a clean tea towel. Chop roughly. In a blender or food processor, blend with the oil until very smooth. Strain through a fine sieve, then through 2 layers of muslin or a paper coffee filter, place in a clean bottle and refrigerate.

2 Put the cumin seeds in a dry, nonstick frying pan and cook over a low heat for 2–3 minutes. Leave to cool, then grind finely in a spice grinder or in a mortar with a pestle.

3 Heat the oil in a large saucepan, add the onion and garlic and cook over a moderate heat for 5 minutes or until softened. Add the peppers, cumin and stock. Bring to the boil. Reduce the heat and simmer for 10 minutes.

4 In a blender or food processor, blend the soup in batches until smooth. Strain through a fine sieve into the pan. Reheat gently. Season to taste with salt and pepper. Serve in warm soup bowls drizzled with the coriander oil.

Red pepper and potato soup

This easy-to-make soup is ideal for a midweek supper. Don't add too much seasoning or you will overpower the flavour of the red peppers. If you are using dried rosemary, you need half the amount of the fresh herb.

1 Heat the oil in a large, heavy-based saucepan, add the garlic, onion and red peppers and cook over a moderate heat for 5 minutes or until softened.

2 Add the stock, rosemary, sugar and tomato purée. Stir well, then add the potatoes. Bring to the boil. Reduce the heat, partially cover and simmer for 40–45 minutes or until the vegetables are very tender.

3 In the blender or food processor, blend the soup in batches until smooth, then transfer it to a clean saucepan. Season to taste with salt and pepper. Reheat gently and serve in warm soup bowls.

15

PREP

50

COOK

4

SERVES

easy

3 tablespoons **olive oil**

1 **garlic clove**, chopped

1 **onion**, chopped

2 **red peppers**, cored, deseeded and chopped

1.2 litres (2 pints) **Vegetable Stock** (see page 19)

½ teaspoon finely chopped **rosemary**

¼ teaspoon **caster sugar**

2 tablespoons **tomato purée**

250 g (8 oz) **potatoes**, chopped

salt and **pepper**

2–3 large **aubergines**, about 1 kg (2 lb) in total

3 tablespoons **olive oil**

1 **red onion**

2 **garlic cloves**, crushed

1.2 litres (2 pints) **Chicken Stock** (see page 17)

200 ml (7 fl oz) **crème fraîche** or **Greek yogurt**

2 tablespoons chopped **mint**

salt and **pepper**

15

PREP

40

COOK

4

SERVES

tasty

Roasted aubergine soup

Aubergines contain a lot of liquid, and grilling or roasting is one way of drying them out before cooking, although they will still need to be pressed to extract more liquid before you use them.

1 Put the aubergines under a preheated hot grill and cook, turning occasionally, for 20 minutes or until the skin is well charred and the flesh has softened. Leave to cool slightly. Cut the aubergines in half, scoop out the flesh and chop.

2 Heat the oil in a large, heavy-based saucepan, add the onion and garlic and cook over a moderate heat for 5 minutes or until softened. Add the chopped aubergine and the stock and cook for 10–15 minutes.

3 In a blender or food processor, blend the soup in batches until smooth. Strain through a sieve into the pan. Reheat gently and season to taste with salt and pepper.

4 Mix the crème fraîche or Greek yogurt with the mint and season to taste with salt and pepper. Serve the soup in warm soup bowls, garnished with a spoonful of the minted crème fraîche or yogurt.

Cream of celeriac soup

10 PREP

30 COOK

Celeriac is a knobbly root vegetable that is a type of celery. Its distinctive flavour makes a delicious soup. Choose firm, small roots – large roots may be hollow or woody inside.

4 SERVES

rich

50 g (2 oz) **butter**

2 **shallots** or 1 **onion**, chopped

1 **garlic clove**, crushed

500 g (1 lb) **celeriac**, diced

900 ml (1½ pints) **Chicken Stock** (see page 17)

300 ml (½ pint) **single cream** or **milk**

75 g (3 oz) whole blanched **almonds**

salt and **pepper**

1 Melt the butter in a large, heavy-based saucepan, add the shallots or onion and garlic and cook over a moderate heat for 5 minutes or until softened. Add the celeriac, cover and cook for 5–10 minutes until the celeriac begins to soften. Add the stock and bring to the boil, then reduce the heat and simmer for 10–15 minutes.

2 In a blender or food processor, blend the soup in batches until smooth, then return it to the pan. Stir in the cream or milk and season to taste with salt and pepper. Reheat gently without boiling.

3 Meanwhile, heat a dry, nonstick frying pan over a moderate heat. Add the almonds and cook, turning frequently, for 5 minutes or until lightly browned and toasted. Tip out of the pan and leave to cool slightly. Grind in a spice grinder or in a mortar with a pestle.

4 Serve the hot soup in warm soup bowls, sprinkled with the ground toasted almonds.

50 g (2 oz) **butter**

1 **onion**, finely chopped

250 g (8 oz) **potatoes**, cut into 1 cm (½ inch) cubes

300 g (10 oz) prepared **watercress**

900 ml (1½ pints) **Vegetable Stock** (see page 19)

300 ml (½ pint) **single cream**

12 **quails' eggs**

50 g (2 oz) **Parmesan cheese**, finely grated, to serve

salt and **pepper**

PREP 10

25

COOK

4

SERVES

party

Watercress soup with quails' eggs

This is a great soup for a special occasion, but it is quick and easy to prepare, so makes an ideal dish for a dinner party. Quails' eggs are a lovely garnish, as well as adding substance to the soup.

1 Melt the butter in a large, heavy-based saucepan, add the onion and cook over a low heat for 8–10 minutes or until softened. Stir in the potatoes and watercress, cover and cook, stirring once or twice, for 3–5 minutes until the watercress has just wilted.

2 Add the stock and season to taste with salt and pepper. Bring to the boil and cook for 6–8 minutes or until the potatoes are tender.

3 In a blender or food processor, blend the soup in batches until smooth. Strain through a sieve into the pan. Add the cream and taste and adjust the seasoning if necessary. Reheat gently without boiling.

4 Meanwhile, poach the eggs in a saucepan of gently simmering water, drain well and put 3 eggs in each bowl. Ladle the soup over the eggs and serve with the grated Parmesan scattered over the top.

Garlic soup with Parmesan dumplings

This hearty soup has an Italian feel, with plenty of garlic and fresh herbs. The dumplings can be prepared in advance, and they will soak up the flavours of the soup as they cook in the liquid.

30*
PREP

55
COOK

4
SERVES

stylish

1 Make the Parmesan dumplings. Put all the ingredients in a bowl and mix to form a firm paste. Season to taste with salt and pepper and nutmeg. Cover and chill for 1 hour. With lightly floured hands, form into 24 small balls, roll in flour and put on a tray.

2 Make the soup. Heat the oil in a large, heavy-based saucepan, add the garlic cloves and onions and cook over a moderate heat for 5 minutes. Reduce the heat, cover tightly and cook for 30–35 minutes until tender. Do not allow to colour.

3 Add the potatoes, bay leaf, thyme, saffron, stock and milk. Season to taste with salt and pepper. Bring to the boil, then reduce the heat and simmer for 20–30 minutes. Add the spinach and cook for 1–2 minutes until wilted.

4 In a blender or food processor, blend the soup in batches until smooth. Strain through a sieve into a clean saucepan. Return to the boil and add the dumplings. Simmer for 3–4 minutes until the dumplings are light and cooked through. Serve immediately.

* Plus 1 hour chilling

5 tablespoons **olive oil**

2 small heads of **garlic**, cloves separated and peeled

2 **onions**, sliced

500 g (1 lb) **potatoes**, diced

1 **bay leaf**

1 sprig of **thyme**

pinch of **saffron threads**

1.2 litres (2 pints) **Chicken Stock** (see page 17)

600 ml (1 pint) **milk**

250 g (8 oz) **spinach**, finely shredded

salt and **pepper**

PARMESAN DUMPLINGS:

175 g (6 oz) **ricotta cheese**

25 g (1 oz) **butter**, softened

25 g (1 oz) **Parmesan cheese**, finely grated

1 teaspoon finely grated **lemon rind**

2 tablespoons **plain flour**

2 **egg yolks**, beaten

grated nutmeg

2 tablespoons **vegetable oil**

1 **onion**, finely chopped

1–2 **garlic cloves**, crushed

1 **red chilli**, deseeded and finely chopped

2.5 cm (1 inch) piece of fresh **root ginger**, peeled and grated

finely grated rind and juice of 1 **lime**

2 large **tomatoes**, skinned and chopped, about 300 g (10 oz)

2 large semi-ripe **plantains**

6 **allspice berries**, crushed

1 sprig of **thyme**

1.2 litres (2 pints) **Chicken Stock** (see page 17)

400 ml (14 fl oz) can **coconut milk**

75 g (3 oz) skinned **Brazil nuts**

salt and **pepper**

20

PREP

60

COOK

6

SERVES

tasty

Coconut and plantain soup

This delicious recipe combines creamy coconut milk with hot red chilli and plantain to produce a soup with a distinctive Creole flavour. The Brazil nuts add an unusual crunchy finish.

1 Heat the oil in a large, heavy-based saucepan, add the onion, garlic, chilli, ginger and lime rind and cook over a low heat for 8–10 minutes or until softened. Add the tomatoes and cook for 5 minutes.

2 Use a small, sharp knife to cut off one end of the plantains. Slit the skins lengthways and unpeel sideways. Chop the flesh. Add to the pan with the allspice, thyme, stock and coconut milk. Season to taste with salt and pepper and bring to the boil. Reduce the heat and simmer for 30 minutes.

3 Meanwhile, spread the Brazil nuts on a baking sheet, then roast in a preheated oven, 160°C (325°F), Gas Mark 3, for 10–15 minutes until lightly golden. Remove from the oven and leave to cool, then chop finely.

4 Remove and discard the thyme from the soup. In a blender or food processor, blend the soup in batches until smooth. Strain through a sieve into the pan. Reheat gently. Add the lime juice. Serve in warm bowls sprinkled with the chopped Brazil nuts.

Chestnut and bacon soup

40
PREP

55
COOK

4
SERVES

feast

If you're using bacon, choose a smoked variety for even more punch. Shallots are much sweeter than regular onions, so opt for these if you can. If you cannot find fresh chestnuts, use 250 g (8 oz) vacuum-packed, cooked chestnuts instead.

1 Cut a slash in the pointed end of each chestnut. Place in a saucepan, cover with cold water and bring to the boil, then reduce the heat and simmer for 2 minutes. Remove from the heat. Using a slotted spoon, lift out one chestnut at a time and remove and discard the outer and inner skins. If the skins are hard to peel, return the pan to the boil and repeat.

2 Melt the butter in a large, heavy-based saucepan, add the pancetta or bacon and cook over a moderate heat, stirring, for 2–3 minutes or until lightly browned. Reduce the heat and add the shallots or onion, fennel and celery. Cook for 6–8 minutes until softened.

3 Add the chestnuts, stock and milk. Season to taste with salt and pepper. Bring to the boil, then reduce the heat and simmer for 30–40 minutes or until the chestnuts are tender.

4 In the blender or food processor, blend the soup in batches until smooth. Strain through a sieve into the pan. Return to the boil. Serve immediately in warm soup bowls.

375 g (12 oz) **chestnuts**

50 g (2 oz) **butter**

75 g (3 oz) rindless **pancetta** or **streaky bacon**, chopped

3 **shallots** or 1 large **onion**, chopped

½ small **fennel bulb**, trimmed and chopped

1 **celery stick**, chopped

600 ml (1 pint) **Chicken Stock** (see page 17)

600 ml (1 pint) **milk**

salt and **pepper**

3 tablespoons **olive oil**

1 **onion**, chopped

250 g (8 oz) **peas**, thawed if frozen

1.2 litres (2 pints) **Chicken Stock** (see page 17)

200 g (7 oz) **arborio rice**

pinch of **caster sugar**

2 tablespoons chopped **flat leaf parsley**

50 g (2 oz) **Parmesan cheese**, finely grated, plus extra to serve

salt and **pepper**

TO GARNISH:

4 slices of **prosciutto**

1 tablespoon **olive oil**

10 PREP

30 COOK

4 SERVES

party

Risi e bisi with frazzled prosciutto

Although it's nice to use fresh peas and pod them yourself, frozen peas are actually just as nutritious. Peas are generally frozen very soon after being picked, so the vitamins are fully preserved.

1 Heat the oil in a large, heavy-based saucepan, add the onion and cook over a moderate heat for 5 minutes or until softened.

2 Add the stock and bring to the boil, then reduce the heat and stir in the rice. If you are using fresh peas, add them now and simmer gently for 5 minutes before adding the rice. Season to taste with salt and pepper and add the sugar. Cover and simmer gently, stirring occasionally, for 15–20 minutes until the rice is tender. If you are using frozen peas, add them after 10–15 minutes.

3 Meanwhile, cut each prosciutto slice in half lengthways. Heat the oil in a large, non-stick frying pan, add the prosciutto strips and cook over a high heat for 10–15 seconds or until crisp. Drain on kitchen paper.

4 Stir the parsley and Parmesan into the hot soup, ladle into warm soup bowls and top with 2 pieces of the frazzled prosciutto. Serve with a small bowl of extra Parmesan to hand round separately.

Bread soup

The title may not sound very appealing, but this is an absolutely delicious and warming soup. It couldn't be easier to make, but will impress your friends.

1 Warm a large tureen or casserole by filling it with boiling water and leaving it to stand for a few minutes.

2 In a blender or food processor, blend the coriander, garlic and salt with 2–4 tablespoons of the oil to make a smooth paste.

3 Discard the water from the tureen or casserole and put the coriander paste in the bottom. Drizzle over the remaining oil, then pour over the measured boiling water and stir in the bread cubes. They will absorb the liquid and become soggy.

4 Poach the eggs in a pan of simmering water. Serve the soup in warm soup bowls, with a poached egg in each, sprinkled with the parsley.

10
PREP

5
COOK

4
SERVES

stylish

25 g (1 oz) fresh **coriander**

4 **garlic cloves**, roughly chopped

1 tablespoon coarse **sea salt**

8 tablespoons extra virgin **olive oil**

1.5 litres (2½ pints) boiling **water**

375 g (12 oz) day-old **ciabatta** or **pugliese**, crusts removed, broken or cut into 2.5 cm (1 inch) cubes

4 **eggs**

2 tablespoons chopped **flat leaf parsley**

pinch of **saffron threads**

125 ml (4 fl oz) boiling **water**

750 g (1½ lb) **mussels**, scrubbed and debearded

175 ml (6 fl oz) **dry white wine**

2 tablespoons **olive oil**

2 **shallots**, finely chopped

1 **garlic clove**, finely chopped

200 ml (7 fl oz) **double cream**

175 g (6 oz) **baby spinach**

15 **basil** leaves, shredded

30

PREP

20

COOK

4

SERVES

herby

Mussel soup with basil and spinach

Mussels take well to many different flavours and soak up the juices they are cooked in. Shallots, garlic and wine are ideal accompaniments, and they are combined here with saffron and spinach.

1 Put the saffron in a small heatproof bowl and pour over the measured boiling water. Leave to soak. Discard any mussels that are broken or open, or that do not close when tapped on a work surface. Put them in a large colander over a bowl.

2 Pour the wine into a large, heavy-based saucepan. Bring to the boil. Add the mussels, cover tightly and cook, shaking the pan frequently, for 2–3 minutes or until all the mussels have opened.

3 Tip the mussels into the colander and remove from their shells, discarding any that have not opened. Strain the mussel liquid through a muslin-lined sieve and set aside.

4 Heat the oil in a saucepan, add the shallots and garlic and cook over a low heat for 5–6 minutes. Add the strained mussel liquid, cream and saffron and its infused liquid and bring to the boil, then reduce the heat and add the spinach, half of the basil and all the mussels. Simmer for 2 minutes, then remove from the heat, stir in the remaining basil and serve.

Crab, asparagus and lemon soup

This luxurious soup requires a freshly cooked crab in the shell. Ask the fishmonger to remove all the white and brown meat for you, but remember to ask for the shell, in order to make the stock. To break the shell into small pieces, put it into a plastic bag and smash with a rolling pin.

1 Put the crab shell in a large, heavy-based saucepan. Cover with 1.2 litres (2 pints) of the measured water. Bring to the boil. Reduce the heat and simmer for 30 minutes. Strain through a fine sieve into a clean saucepan.

2 Bring the remaining water to the boil in a separate saucepan with a pinch of salt. Add the asparagus and simmer for 2–3 minutes until just tender. Drain, reserving the liquid, refresh in cold water and drain again.

3 Return the crab stock to the boil. Add the asparagus water and the rice and simmer gently for 12–15 minutes until tender.

4 In a bowl, mix together the cream cheese, 5 tablespoons of the brown crab meat, and salt and pepper and cayenne pepper to taste. Spread each toast slice with the mixture.

5 In a small bowl, mix together the egg yolks and lemon juice. Whisk in a ladleful of the stock. Whisk the egg mixture into the pan. Do not boil. Add the asparagus and white crab meat and heat through. Serve sprinkled with chervil and accompanied by the toasts.

20
PREP

60
COOK

4
SERVES

posh

1 freshly cooked **crab**, about 750 g (1½ lb), white and brown meat removed and shell broken into small pieces

1.65 litres (2¾ pints) **water**

250 g (8 oz) fine young **asparagus**, cut into 5 cm (2 inch) pieces

75 g (3 oz) **white long-grain rice**

50 g (2 oz) **cream cheese**

cayenne pepper

8 thin slices of French **bread**, toasted

3 **egg yolks**

2 tablespoons **lemon juice**

salt and **pepper**

sprigs of **chervil**, to garnish

oriental

300 ml (½ pint) **Chicken Stock** (see page 17)

3 **kaffir lime leaves**, torn in half

½ **lemon grass stalk**, obliquely sliced

2.5 cm (1 inch) piece of **galangal**, peeled and thinly sliced

100 ml (3½ fl oz) **coconut milk**

4 tablespoons **Thai fish sauce**

1 teaspoon **palm sugar** or **light muscovado sugar**

3 tablespoons **lime juice**

125 g (4 oz) **chicken**, skinned and cut into bite-sized pieces

2 tablespoons **chilli oil** or 2 **small chillies**, thinly sliced (optional)

10

PREP

10

COOK

4

SERVES

easy

Chicken and coconut milk soup

This quantity of soup is enough for 1 large bowl of soup shared between 4 people or 4 small, individual bowls. If you would like to serve the soup as a first course on its own, in Western style, just double the quantities.

1 Pour the stock into a large, heavy-based saucepan and bring to the boil. Stir in the lime leaves, lemon grass and galangal. Reduce the heat to a simmer. Add the coconut milk, fish sauce, sugar and lime juice and stir well, then add the chicken pieces and simmer for 5 minutes.

2 Just before serving, add the chilli oil or chillies (if using) and stir again. Serve the soup immediately in warm soup bowls.

Noodle soup with chicken

PREP 15

This soup is sufficient on its own for a light meal for 4 people. If you wish to serve it as part of a Thai meal, you should halve or even quarter the quantities.

COOK 15

1 Put the stock, star anise, cinnamon stick pieces, pickled garlic, vinegar, fish sauce, coriander, sugar and soy sauce in a large, heavy-based saucepan and bring slowly to the boil. Add the chicken pieces and simmer for 4 minutes. Add the pak choi and bean sprouts and simmer for a further 2 minutes.

SERVES 4

2 Meanwhile, make the crispy shallots. Heat the oil in a wok or deep frying pan. Finely chop the shallots. Add to the hot oil and cook, stirring, for 40 seconds or until sizzling and golden. Remove with a slotted spoon and spread out on kitchen paper to drain.

classic

3 Divide the rice sticks between 4 large soup bowls and ladle over the soup. Sprinkle the coriander leaves on top and garnish with the crispy shallots.

1.2 litres (2 pints) **Chicken Stock** (see page 17)

1 **star anise**

8 cm (3 inch) piece of **cinnamon stick**, broken

2 bulbs **pickled garlic**, finely chopped

4 tablespoons **pickled garlic vinegar**

125 ml (4 fl oz) **Thai fish sauce**

8 fresh **coriander roots**, finely chopped

4 teaspoons **palm sugar**

4 teaspoons **soy sauce**

200 g (7 oz) **chicken**, skinned and diced

125 g (4 oz) **pak choi**, roughly chopped

50 g (2 oz) **bean sprouts**

200 g (7 oz) **rice sticks**, cooked

15 g (½ oz) fresh **coriander**

CRISPY SHALLOTS:

about 750 ml (1¼ pints) **groundnut oil**

25 g (1 oz) **shallots**

200 ml (7 fl oz) can **coconut milk**, shaken

200 ml (7 fl oz) **Chicken Stock** (see page 17)

2 **lemon grass stalks** (white part only), each 12 cm (5 inches) long and bruised

5 cm (2 inches) fresh **galangal**, peeled and cut into several pieces

15 **black peppercorns**, crushed

400 g (13 oz) boneless, skinless **chicken breast**

1 tablespoon **Thai fish sauce**

1 tablespoon **palm sugar**

150 g (5 oz) **mixed mushrooms**, such as oyster, shiitake or button

200 g (7 oz) **cherry tomatoes**

2–3 tablespoons **lime juice** or **lemon juice**

5 **kaffir lime leaves**, torn in half

3–5 small **red and green chillies**, bruised

fresh **coriander**, to garnish

15

PREP

15

COOK

4

SERVES

fresh

Chicken, coconut and galangal soup

Here is a classic Thai dish that is enjoyed by adults and children alike. The galangal and lemon grass give it plenty of flavour, but it is not too hot.

1 Put the coconut milk, stock, lemon grass, galangal and peppercorns in a large, heavy-based saucepan or wok and slowly bring to the boil.

2 Slice the chicken, then add to the pan with the fish sauce and sugar. Reduce the heat and simmer, stirring constantly, for 5 minutes or until the chicken is cooked through.

3 Halve the mushrooms if they are large and remove and discard the hard stalks. Add to the pan with the tomatoes and simmer for 2–3 minutes, taking care that the tomatoes do not lose their shape. Add the lime or lemon juice, lime leaves and chillies for the last few seconds of cooking.

4 Serve the soup immediately in warm soup bowls, garnished with a few coriander leaves.

Thai chicken and coconut soup

Thai red curry paste adds the essential fiery heat to this soup, while the kaffir lime leaves add a sharp citrus punch. You should be able to find fresh kaffir lime leaves in Asian stores and larger supermarkets. The leaves can be stored in the refrigerator for up to a month or in the freezer for months at a time.

1 Heat the oil in a wok or deep, nonstick frying pan, add the curry paste and stir-fry for 1 minute until sizzling. Add the chicken and lime leaves and stir-fry for 1 minute until evenly coated in the curry paste.

2 Add the stock and bring to the boil. Reduce the heat, cover and simmer for 15 minutes. Add all the remaining ingredients to the pan and simmer gently for a further 2–3 minutes.

3 Spoon the soup into warm soup bowls and serve topped with basil leaves, sliced red chilli and shredded lime leaves.

15
PREP

20
COOK

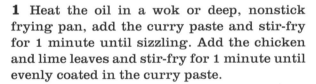

4
SERVES

hot

2 tablespoons **vegetable oil**

1–2 tablespoons **Thai red curry paste**

750 g (1½ lb) boneless, skinless **chicken breast**, diced

8 **kaffir lime leaves**

600 ml (1 pint) **Chicken Stock** (see page 17)

200 g (7 oz) **French beans**, trimmed and halved

1 **red pepper**, cored, deseeded and sliced

400 ml (14 fl oz) can **coconut milk**

1 tablespoon **Thai fish sauce**

TO GARNISH:

Thai basil or ordinary **basil** leaves

sliced **red chilli**

shredded **kaffir lime leaves**

600 ml (1 pint) **Chicken Stock** (see page 17)

2 **garlic cloves**, sliced

100 g (3½) oz **minced pork**

3 dried **black fungus**, soaked in hot water for 20 minutes, drained and sliced

2 tablespoons **light soy sauce**

1 tablespoon **Thai fish sauce**

50 g (2 oz) dried **rice vermicelli**, soaked in hot water for 15–20 minutes and cut into 5 cm (2 inch) lengths

10*

PREP

10

COOK

4

SERVES

simple

Pork ball and black fungus soup

This soup is so simple and quick to prepare. Soak the black fungus and vermicelli in advance so that everything is ready to go when you want to eat.

1 Heat the stock in a wok or large, heavy-based saucepan and add the garlic.

2 Shape the pork into small round balls. Drop them into the simmering stock and cook for 5 minutes.

3 Add the black fungus, soy sauce, fish sauce and rice vermicelli and simmer for about 2 minutes. Serve immediately in warm soup bowls.

* Plus 20 minutes soaking

Pork and bamboo shoot soup

This recipe uses plenty of garlic, so it might not be the best choice for a romantic dinner! However, it should keep those colds at bay, and the soup isn't dominated by garlic; it blends well with the pork.

10

PREP

12

COOK

4

SERVES

tasty

1 Heat the stock in a wok or large, heavy-based saucepan and add the peppercorns and crushed and chopped garlic.

2 Meanwhile, mix the pork with the soy sauce and pepper, then shape into small balls. Drop the balls into the simmering stock and cook for 4 minutes.

3 Add the bamboo shoots and simmer gently for 5 minutes. Add the fish sauce and stir well. Serve in warm soup bowls, garnished with the spring onion and coriander leaves.

450 ml (¾ pint) **Chicken Stock** (see page 17)

10 **black peppercorns**, crushed

7 garlic cloves, 2 crushed, 5 roughly chopped

125 g (4 oz) **minced pork**

1½ tablespoons **light soy sauce**

pinch of **pepper**

100 g (3½) oz **bamboo shoots**

3 tablespoons **Thai fish sauce**

TO GARNISH:

1 **spring onion**, obliquely sliced

fresh **coriander**

175 g (6 oz) fresh **egg noodles**

1 teaspoon **garlic oil**

2 **choi sum**, sliced

5 g (¼ oz) **spring onions**, thinly sliced

1 tablespoon **light soy sauce**

5 g (¼ oz) fresh **coriander**

pinch of **pepper**

200 g (7 oz) **roast pork**, sliced

600 ml (1 pint) **Chicken Stock** (see page 17)

DIPPING SAUCE:

4 tablespoons distilled **white vinegar**

2–3 tablespoons **Thai fish sauce**

1 large **red chilli**, sliced

15

PREP

10

COOK

4

SERVES

stylish

Pork and noodle soup

Choi sum is a type of Chinese green leafy vegetable. If you cannot find it, you can use other oriental greens, such as pak choi, instead. For a really authentic dish, use pork that has first been marinaded in a red pork sauce, available from oriental supermarkets.

1 Bring a large saucepan of water to the boil, add the egg noodles and boil for 2–3 minutes, untangling while boiling. Drain well and return to the pan. Add the garlic oil and toss to coat, to prevent sticking together.

2 Meanwhile, make the dipping sauce. Combine all the ingredients in a small bowl.

3 Blanch the choi sum in a separate saucepan of boiling water for 1 minute, then drain.

4 Put the cooked noodles in a large, heatproof serving bowl. Add the choi sum, spring onions, soy sauce, coriander and pepper. Arrange the pork slices on the top.

5 Heat the stock in a saucepan to boiling point, then pour over the pork, noodles and vegetables. Serve the soup immediately with the dipping sauce.

Pork ball and tofu soup

15

PREP

Tofu is believed to have many health benefits, and it is a staple ingredient in many Asian cuisines. It's very versatile and, although fairly bland on its own, can absorb other flavours easily.

10

COOK

1 Heat the stock with the chopped and halved garlic, pepper and coriander in a large, heavy-based saucepan.

2 Meanwhile, make the pork balls. Mix the pork with the soy sauce and pepper, then shape into small balls. Drop the balls into the simmering stock and cook for 4 minutes.

3 Add the tofu, laver and soy sauce, stir for 30 seconds, then serve the soup in warm soup bowls, garnished with coriander leaves.

4

SERVES

quick

600 ml (1 pint) **Chicken Stock** (see page 17)

5 **garlic cloves**, 1 finely chopped, 4 halved

½ teaspoon **pepper**

8 fresh **coriander roots**, roughly chopped

200 g (7 oz) **silken tofu**, cut into 2.5 cm (1 inch) slices

1 sheet roasted **laver**, torn into shreds

2 tablespoons **light soy sauce**

fresh **coriander**, to garnish

PORK BALLS:

65 g (2½ oz) **minced pork**

1 tablespoon **light soy sauce**

½ teaspoon **pepper**

4 dried, long **red chillies**, about 12 cm (5 inches) long, or 4 dried, small **red chillies**, about 5 cm (2 inches) long

7 **shallots**, roughly chopped

4 **garlic cloves**, roughly chopped

1 teaspoon **shrimp paste**

1.2 litres (2 pints) **Vegetable Stock** (see page 19)

375 g (12 oz) **minced pork**

375 g (12 oz) **snake beans**, cut into 2.5 cm (1 inch) pieces

2 tablespoons **Thai fish sauce**

5 tablespoons **lemon juice**

15

PREP

8

COOK

6

SERVES

exotic

Sour pork soup with snake beans

In Thailand, this slightly hot and sour soup is a popular addition to a main meal. Snake beans are narrow, round and stringless beans, 30–90 cm (12–36 inches) long, and can be found in Thai or oriental supermarkets. Green beans can be used instead if you have trouble finding them.

1 Cut off the stalks of the chillies, then slit the chillies lengthways with a sharp knife. Remove and discard all the seeds and chop the flesh roughly. Put it in a heatproof bowl, cover with hot water and leave to soak for 2 minutes or until softened, then drain.

2 Put the chillies, shallots, garlic and shrimp paste in a mortar and pound with a pestle to form a smooth paste.

3 Pour the stock into a large, heavy-based saucepan and bring to the boil. Stir in the chilli paste, then reduce the heat to moderate.

4 Shape the pork into small balls. Drop the balls into the simmering stock with the beans, fish sauce and lemon juice. Cook for 4–5 minutes. Spoon the soup into a serving bowl and serve immediately.

Rice soup with minced pork

15
PREP

10
COOK

If you prefer, you could use chicken or prawns instead of the minced pork. If you cannot find Chinese cabbage, spinach makes a good alternative.

4

SERVES

filling

1 Put the coriander roots, garlic and pepper in a mortar and pound with a pestle to form a smooth paste.

2 Transfer the coriander paste to a bowl and combine it with the pork.

3 Put the stock in a large, heavy-based saucepan and bring to the boil. Add the soy sauce, preserved radish (if using) and rice.

4 Shape the pork mixture into small balls. Drop the balls into the simmering soup and cook for 3 minutes.

5 Add the ginger and Chinese cabbage. Cook for a further 1–2 minutes. Spoon the soup into a serving bowl. Garnish with the spring onions and coriander leaves. Season to taste with pepper and serve immediately.

3 fresh **coriander roots**, roughly chopped

3 **garlic cloves**, roughly chopped

¼ teaspoon **white pepper**

400 g (13 oz) **minced pork**

1.8 litres (3 pints) **Vegetable Stock** (see page 19)

3 tablespoons **light soy sauce**

1 tablespoon **preserved radish**, finely chopped (optional)

625 g (1¼ lb) boiled **jasmine rice**

2.5 cm (1 inch) piece of fresh **root ginger**, peeled and thinly sliced

50 g (2 oz) **Chinese cabbage leaves**, roughly chopped

TO SERVE:

2 **spring onions**, finely chopped

fresh **coriander**

white pepper

1.5 litres (2½ pints) **Chicken Stock** (see page 17)

2 **lemon grass stalks**, bruised

small piece of fresh **root ginger**, peeled and thinly sliced

2 tablespoons **light soy sauce**

2 tablespoons **lime juice**

2 teaspoons **soft dark brown sugar**

125 g (4 oz) dried flat **rice noodles**

275 g (9 oz) **sirloin steak**, sliced

TO SERVE:

150 g (5 oz) **bean sprouts**

1 **red chilli**, thinly sliced

handful of **Thai basil**

handful of **mint**

PREP 15

COOK 20

SERVES 4

classic

Vietnamese beef pho

This is the national dish of Vietnam: a spicy, fragrant broth served with rice noodles, bean sprouts, aromatic herbs and slices of rare beef. Save this comforting dish for a night when it's cold and raining outside, and you feel in need of a spiritual and physical uplift.

1 Put the stock, lemon grass, ginger, soy sauce, lime juice and sugar in a large, heavy-based saucepan and bring to the boil. Reduce the heat and simmer gently for 10 minutes.

2 Using a slotted spoon, remove the lemon grass and ginger and discard. Add the rice noodles and cook according to the packet instructions, adding the sliced steak for the last 2–3 minutes.

3 Spoon the pho into warm soup bowls, top with the bean sprouts, chilli, basil and mint and serve immediately.

Hot and sour prawn soup

10

PREP

Hot and sour is a common combination in Chinese food, much like sweet and sour. Here, the heat comes from the chilli oil, while lime juice offers the 'sour' element of the recipe.

20

COOK

1 Put the stock, lime leaves, lemon grass, galangal, sugar, lime juice and chilli oil or chopped chillies in a large wok or heavy-based saucepan and bring to the boil. Reduce the heat and simmer gently for 15 minutes.

2 Add the prawns just before serving; they will turn pink in a few seconds and will be cooked through after 1 minute.

3 Season to taste with salt and pepper and serve the soup in one large bowl or individual bowls, garnished with coriander sprigs.

4

SERVES

hot

1.2 litres (2 pints) **Fish Stock** (see page 16)

4 **kaffir lime leaves**, torn in half

1 **lemon grass stalk**, thinly and obliquely sliced

2.5 cm (1 inch) piece of **galangal**, peeled and sliced

1 tablespoon **palm sugar** or **light muscovado sugar**

5 tablespoons **lime juice**

2 tablespoons **chilli oil** or 12 small **green chillies**, chopped

12–16 raw peeled **prawns**

salt and **pepper**

sprigs of fresh **coriander**, to garnish

125 g (4 oz) dried **soba noodles**

2 teaspoons **sesame oil**

1 bunch of **spring onions**, sliced

2 **pak choi**, shredded

1.8 litres (3 pints) hot **Vegetable Stock** (see page 19)

4 tablespoons **sake**

2 tablespoons **dark soy sauce**

125 g (4 oz) **bean sprouts**

vegetable oil, for deep-frying

12 raw **tiger prawns**, peeled and deveined

2 sheets of **nori**, shredded

TEMPURA:

1 **egg yolk**

50 g (2 oz) **plain flour**

100 ml (3½ fl oz) iced **water**

20

PREP

10

COOK

4

SERVES

stylish

Noodle soup with prawn tempura

Nori is a type of dried seaweed that you will usually find wrapped around sushi. It is now widely available in supermarkets and is used here as a garnish.

1 Cook the soba noodles according to the packet instructions. Drain well.

2 Heat the sesame oil in a large wok, add the spring onions and pak choi and stir-fry for 1 minute. Add the stock, sake and soy sauce and simmer gently for 5 minutes. Stir in the bean sprouts.

3 Meanwhile, make the tempura. In a bowl, briefly whisk together the egg yolk, flour and water to make a slightly lumpy batter. Heat the vegetable oil in a separate wok, a deep, heavy-based saucepan or deep-fat fryer to 180–190°C (350–375°F), or until a cube of bread browns in 30 seconds. Dip the prawns in the batter, then drop them into the hot oil and cook for 3 minutes or until golden. Remove with a slotted spoon and drain on kitchen paper.

4 Spoon the noodles into warm soup bowls, add the soup and top with the prawns and strips of nori. Serve immediately.

Hot and sour soup with seafood

This is one of the most popular soups in Thai cuisine. If you prefer, you can include chicken, beef or lamb instead of the seafood.

30
PREP

8
COOK

4
SERVES

fresh

1 Put the stock, lemon grass, coriander and fish sauce in a saucepan and bring to the boil.

2 Reduce the heat, add the seafood and simmer for 2 minutes.

3 Cut any large mushrooms into quarters and add the mushrooms, onion, chillies, tomatoes, torn lime leaves and lime or lemon juice to the pan. Cook for 2–3 minutes, taking care not to let the tomatoes lose their shape.

4 Turn the soup into a serving bowl, garnish with a few thinly sliced lime leaves and serve.

900 ml (1½ pints) **Fish Stock** (see page 16)

3 **lemon grass stalks** (white part only), each 12 cm (5 inches) long, bruised

5 fresh **coriander roots**, bruised

2 tablespoons **Thai fish sauce**

625 g (1¼ lb) prepared mixed seafood, such as raw **prawns**, **squid**, **white fish** fillet (cod or sea bass), **scallops** and **mussels**, cut into bite-sized pieces

125 g (4 oz) **straw mushrooms**

1 **onion**, quartered

4–5 small **red and green chillies**, slightly crushed

12 **cherry tomatoes**

5 **kaffir lime leaves**, torn in half, plus extra, thinly sliced, to garnish

3 tablespoons **lime juice** or **lemon juice**

50 g (2 oz) **mixed mushrooms**, such as oyster, chestnut and shiitake

1.8 litres (3 pints) **Vegetable Stock** (see page 19)

4 tablespoons **light soy sauce**

1 tablespoon **preserved radish**, finely chopped (optional)

625 g (1¼ lb) boiled **jasmine rice**

300 g (10 oz) prepared mixed seafood, such as raw **prawns**, **squid**, **white fish** fillet (cod or sea bass) and **scallops**, cut into bite-sized pieces

2.5 cm (1 inch) piece of fresh **root ginger**, peeled and thinly sliced

white pepper

TO GARNISH:

2 **spring onions**, thinly and obliquely sliced

fresh **coriander**

30 PREP

10 COOK

4 SERVES

party

Thai rice soup with seafood

To eat in Thailand is to eat rice, and it will come as no surprise to find rice in desserts, or, as here, in soup.

1 Cut any large mushrooms in half and remove and discard the hard stalks.

2 Put the stock in a large, heavy-based saucepan and bring to the boil. Add the soy sauce, preserved radish (if using) and rice, reduce the heat and simmer for 2–3 minutes.

3 Add the seafood, mushrooms and ginger and simmer for 2–3 minutes.

4 Spoon the soup into a large serving bowl, then garnish with the spring onions and coriander leaves. Season to taste with pepper and serve immediately.

Fragrant tofu and noodle soup

Lemon grass can be added whole or halved to flavour a dish, or it is sometimes finely chopped to become an ingredient. Before using it, remove the very tough outer layers of the stalks.

15* PREP

10 COOK

2 SERVES

herby

1 Put the tofu on a plate covered with kitchen paper. Leave to stand for 10 minutes to drain.

2 Heat the oil in a wok or large, nonstick frying pan until hot, add the tofu and stir-fry for 2–3 minutes or until golden brown. Remove with a slotted spoon and drain on kitchen paper.

3 Meanwhile, soak the rice noodles in a saucepan of boiling water for 2 minutes, then drain well.

4 Put the stock in a large, heavy-based saucepan, add the ginger, garlic, lime leaves and lemon grass and bring to the boil. Reduce the heat, add the tofu, noodles, spinach or pak choi, bean sprouts and chillies and heat through for 2 minutes. Stir in the coriander and fish sauce, then pour into warm, deep soup bowls to serve. Serve with lime wedges and chilli sauce.

125 g (4 oz) firm **tofu**, diced

1 tablespoon **sesame oil**

75 g (3 oz) dried fine **rice noodles**

600 ml (1 pint) **Vegetable Stock** (see page 19)

2.5 cm (1 inch) piece of fresh **root ginger**, peeled and thickly sliced

1 large **garlic clove**, thickly sliced

3 **kaffir lime leaves**, torn in half

2 **lemon grass stalks**, halved

handful of **spinach** or **pak choi** leaves

50 g (2 oz) **bean sprouts**

1–2 **red chillies**, deseeded and thinly sliced

2 tablespoons fresh **coriander**, roughly chopped

1 tablespoon **Thai fish sauce**

TO SERVE:

lime wedges

chilli sauce

* Plus 10 minutes draining

Stuffed bitter melon soup

2 **bitter melons**, about 25 cm (10 inches) long

250 g (8 oz) block **ready-fried tofu**, diced

½ **onion**, chopped

25 g (1 oz) dried **black fungus**, soaked in hot water for 20 minutes and drained

1 fresh **coriander root**

2 **garlic cloves**, halved

2 tablespoons **groundnut oil**

2 **eggs**

2 teaspoons **light soy sauce**

1 teaspoon **pepper**

1 teaspoon **salt**

750 ml (1¼ pints) **Vegetable Stock** (see page 19)

fresh **coriander** leaves, to serve

CRISPY GARLIC:

about 750 ml (1¼ pints) **groundnut oil**

25 g (1 oz) **garlic**, finely chopped

15*

PREP

15

COOK

4

SERVES

exotic

* Plus 20 minutes soaking

This is a very unusual recipe, which uses the soup as a stock to pour over stuffed melon segments. Asian supermarkets will stock the more specialist ingredients.

1 Make the crispy garlic. Heat the oil in a wok or deep frying pan, add the garlic and cook, stirring, for 40 seconds or until sizzling and golden. Remove with a slotted spoon and spread on kitchen paper to drain.

2 Cut the ends off the bitter melons and discard, then cut them crossways into 4 equal pieces. Carefully remove the seeds and pith from each piece of melon, then set aside.

3 In a blender or food processor, blend the tofu, onion, black fungus, coriander and garlic. Heat the oil in a wok, add the blended mixture, 1 egg, the soy sauce, pepper and salt and stir-fry for 1–2 minutes. Remove from the heat, turn into a bowl and leave to cool.

4 Add the remaining egg to the tofu mixture to bind, then use to stuff the melon pieces. Steam in a steamer for 10 minutes until cooked. Meanwhile, simmer the stock.

5 Put the melon in a serving bowl. Ladle over the hot stock. Garnish with coriander leaves and serve sprinkled with the crispy garlic.

Clear soup with black fungus

This soup couldn't be simpler to make. Slice the spring onions on the diagonal for an authentic look and serve as part of a Chinese buffet dinner.

1 Pour the stock into a large, heavy-based saucepan and bring to the boil. Add all the remaining ingredients, except the crispy garlic, then reduce the heat and simmer for 2 minutes.

2 Ladle the soup into warm soup bowls and serve hot, garnished with the crispy garlic.

10*

PREP

7

COOK

4

SERVES

quick

600 ml (1 pint) **Vegetable Stock** (see page 19)

1 teaspoon **caster sugar**

½ teaspoon **light soy sauce**

125 g (4 oz) dried **black fungus**, soaked in hot water for 20 minutes, drained and chopped

25 g (1 oz) **celery**, leaf and stalk, finely chopped

25 g (1 oz) **spring onions**, sliced lengthways

salt and **pepper**, to taste

1 teaspoon **Crispy Garlic** (see page 208), to garnish

* Plus 20 minutes soaking

125 g (4 oz) **cucumber**, roughly chopped

1 **onion**, halved

2 **garlic cloves**, halved

50 g (2 oz) **white cabbage**, chopped

600 ml (1 pint) **water**

125 g (4 oz) dried **bean thread noodles**, soaked and drained

25 g (1 oz) dried **tofu sheets**, soaked, drained and torn

15 g (½ oz) dried **lily flowers**, soaked and drained

1 teaspoon **salt**

1 teaspoon **caster sugar**

½ teaspoon **light soy sauce**

2 large dried **shiitake mushrooms**, soaked, drained and thinly sliced

chopped **celery leaves**, to garnish

PREP

COOK

SERVES

Glass noodle soup

A firm favourite on restaurant menus, this is an easy dish to prepare, despite having a number of ingredients. Soak the noodles, tofu, flowers and mushrooms in advance, according to the packet instructions.

1 In a blender or food processor, blend the cucumber, onion, garlic and cabbage for 15 seconds. Turn the mixture into a saucepan and add the measured water. Bring to the boil, then reduce the heat and simmer, stirring occasionally, for 2 minutes.

2 Strain the stock into a large, heavy-based saucepan and add the bean thread noodles, tofu, lily flowers, salt, sugar and soy sauce. Stir, then cook over a moderate heat for about 3 minutes. Taste and adjust the seasoning if necessary.

3 Pour the soup into a serving bowl and arrange the mushroom slices in the centre. Sprinkle with chopped celery leaves and serve immediately.

* Plus 2–3 hours soaking

Banana soup

Banana and chilli make a surprisingly good pairing. Although naturally sweet, the other ingredients add the savoury element, and the soup is well balanced.

15

PREP

10

COOK

4

SERVES

exotic

1 Heat the oil in a large, heavy-based saucepan, add the sliced spring onion and garlic and stir-fry over a high heat for 2 minutes. Add all the other ingredients, in order, then simmer for 5 minutes.

2 If liked, the soup can be blended. Set aside about one-quarter of the banana and chilli slices. In a blender or food processor, blend the remaining soup in batches until smooth, then return it to the pan. Add the reserved banana and chilli slices and heat through without boiling for 3 minutes.

3 Serve the soup hot, garnished with coriander, lime quarters and spring onion strips.

1 tablespoon **groundnut oil**

50 g (2 oz) **spring onions**, including green shoots, sliced

25 g (1 oz) **garlic**, sliced

200 ml (7 fl oz) **coconut milk**

400 ml (14 fl oz) hot **Vegetable Stock** (see page 19)

¼ teaspoon **white pepper**

3 teaspoons **fish sauce** or **light soy sauce**

¼ teaspoon **salt**

½ teaspoon **caster sugar**

1 large **banana**, peeled and cut obliquely into thin slices

1 large **red chilli**, obliquely sliced

TO GARNISH:

fresh **coriander**

2 **limes**, quartered

spring onions, cut into strips

about 750 ml (1¼ pints) **groundnut oil**

250 g (8 oz) block **ready-fried tofu**, diced

750 ml (1¼ pints) **water**

1 **lemon grass stalk**

3 **kaffir lime leaves**

2.5 cm (1 inch) piece of **galangal**, peeled and sliced

1½ teaspoons **salt**

1 teaspoon **caster sugar**

10 small **green chillies**, chopped

3 tablespoons **lime juice**

1 teaspoon **fish sauce** or **light soy sauce**

2 **spring onions**, sliced lengthways

1 **carrot**, cut into matchsticks

1 **shiitake mushroom**, thinly sliced

handful of fresh **coriander**, to garnish

15

PREP

20

COOK

4

SERVES

light

Tofu soup

Tofu changes texture considerably when it is deep-fried, and it takes on the flavour from the oil, in this case groundnut oil. This also helps it to hold its shape when it has been added to the soup.

1 Heat the oil in a wok or deep frying pan, add the tofu and cook, stirring, for 3 minutes or until golden on all sides. Remove with a slotted spoon and drain on kitchen paper.

2 Put the measured water, lemon grass, lime leaves, galangal, salt and sugar in a large saucepan and bring to the boil. Continue to boil for 10 minutes. Remove from the heat.

3 Add the chillies, lime juice, fish or soy sauce, spring onions, carrot and mushroom and simmer for about 4 minutes. Add the tofu and simmer for a further 2 minutes. Serve hot, garnished with the coriander.

Hot sour soup with mooli radish

If you don't have any homemade red curry paste prepared, you can make this dish with a bought paste, which is available in most supermarkets. You will see it a lot in Thai recipes, as it forms the base of many soups and curries.

5
PREP

10
COOK

4
SERVES

simple

1 Heat the stock in a large, heavy-based saucepan. Add the curry paste and stir until well combined. Bring the soup to the boil and add the mooli. Reduce the heat and add the salt, sugar, fish or soy sauce and tamarind water. Simmer for a few minutes until the mooli slices are tender.

2 Put the spinach in the bottom of a large serving bowl, then pour the hot soup over the top. Serve immediately.

750 ml (1¼ pints) **Vegetable Stock** (see page 19)

1 tablespoon **red curry paste**

1 **mooli radish**, peeled and sliced

2 teaspoons **salt**

40 g (1½ oz) **palm sugar** or **light muscovado sugar**

2 tablespoons **fish sauce** or **light soy sauce**

3 tablespoons **tamarind water**

50 g (2 oz) **spinach**, leaves and stalks, torn

2 tablespoons **sunflower oil**

4 **spring onions**, finely chopped

4 **curry leaves** or 1 **bay leaf**

400 g (13 oz) can chopped **tomatoes**

1 teaspoon **salt**

1 **garlic clove**, crushed

1 teaspoon **black peppercorns**, roughly crushed

3 tablespoons chopped fresh **coriander**

500 ml (17 fl oz) **Vegetable Stock** (see page 19)

200 ml (7 fl oz) **single cream**

hot crusty **bread**, to serve

PREP

20

COOK

4

SERVES

herby

Tomato and coriander soup

This fragrant tomato soup is infused with plenty of fresh coriander. Curry leaves give an Asian twist, while the cream thickens and cools it. Garnish with sprigs of coriander just before serving.

1 Heat the oil in a large, heavy-based saucepan, add the spring onions, curry leaves or bay leaf and tomatoes and cook over a moderate heat for 2–3 minutes.

2 Add the salt, garlic, crushed peppercorns, coriander and stock. Stir well and bring to the boil. Reduce the heat, cover and simmer gently for 10 minutes.

3 Stir in the cream and heat through gently without boiling for 1–2 minutes.

4 Ladle the soup into warm soup bowls and serve immediately with hot crusty bread.

Black bean soup with soba noodles

Soba noodles, a traditional ingredient in Japanese cooking, are made of buckwheat and wholemeal flour, giving them a nutty flavour but without the dryness of many wholewheat pastas.

1 Cook the soba noodles in a large saucepan of boiling water for about 5 minutes or until just tender.

2 Meanwhile, heat the oil in a large, heavy-based saucepan, add the spring onions and garlic and stir-fry over a moderate heat for 1 minute.

3 Add the chilli, ginger, black bean sauce and stock and bring to the boil. Stir in the pak choi or spring greens, soy sauce, sugar and peanuts, reduce the heat and simmer gently for 4 minutes.

4 Drain the noodles, then pile them into warm serving bowls. Ladle over the hot soup and serve immediately.

15
PREP

5
COOK

4
SERVES

hearty

200 g (7 oz) dried **soba noodles**

2 tablespoons **groundnut oil** or **vegetable oil**

1 bunch of **spring onions**, sliced

2 **garlic cloves**, roughly chopped

1 **red chilli**, deseeded and sliced

3.5 cm (1½ inch) piece of fresh **root ginger**, peeled and grated

125 ml (4 fl oz) **black bean sauce** or **black bean stir-fry sauce**

750 ml (1¼ pints) **Vegetable Stock** (see page 19)

200 g (7 oz) **pak choi** or **spring greens**, shredded

2 teaspoons **light soy sauce**

1 teaspoon **caster sugar**

50 g (2 oz) raw, unsalted **shelled peanuts**

750 ml (1¼ pints) **Vegetable Stock** (see page 19)

2 tablespoons **miso paste**

125 g (4 oz) **shiitake mushrooms**, sliced

200 g (7 oz) firm **tofu**, diced

crusty **bread**, to serve

PREP

COOK

SERVES

quick

Quick and easy miso soup

This is a very quick and easy recipe, which can be served as an appetizer for a meal or for a light lunch or snack. In restaurants, miso soup is usually sipped straight from the bowl.

1 Pour the stock into a large, heavy-based saucepan and heat until simmering.

2 Add the miso paste, mushrooms and tofu and simmer gently for 5 minutes. Serve the soup hot with crusty bread.

Bean sprouts and tofu soup

15 *
PREP

10
COOK

4
SERVES

tasty

You can use minced prawns instead of chicken or pork, if you prefer. If you are unable to find coriander roots, use 1 table-spoon finely chopped fresh coriander leaves. Big head bean sprouts are available in most oriental supermarkets.

1 In a bowl, mix together the meat, garlic, coriander and black fungus.

2 Clean the bean sprouts and discard the tails. Drain the tofu and cut it into 2.5 cm (1 inch) cubes.

3 Pour the stock into a large, heavy-based saucepan and bring to the boil. Stir in the soy sauce, then reduce the heat.

4 Shape the meat mixture into small balls. Drop the balls into the simmering stock and cook for 2–3 minutes.

5 Add the tofu and bean sprouts and simmer for a further 2–3 minutes, taking care not to let the tofu cubes lose their shape. Spoon the soup into a serving bowl and season to taste with pepper. Serve immediately, garnished with the spring onions.

150 g (5 oz) **minced chicken** or **minced pork**

3 **garlic cloves**, finely chopped

2–3 fresh **coriander roots**, finely chopped

10 dried **black fungus**, soaked in hot water for 20 minutes, drained and finely chopped

150 g (5 oz) **big head bean sprouts**

375 g (12 oz) firm **tofu**

1.8 litres (3 pints) **Chicken Stock** (see page 17)

2 tablespoons **light soy sauce**

white pepper

2 **spring onions**, thinly sliced, to garnish

* Plus 20 minutes soaking

45 wonton wrappers

1.5 litres (2½ pints) **Chicken Stock** (see page 17)

8 **Chinese leaves**, shredded

2 **spring onions**, sliced, to garnish

STUFFING:

100 g (3½ oz) **minced pork** or **minced chicken**

100 g (3½ oz) raw peeled **prawns**, roughly chopped

2 **spring onions**, thinly sliced

2 slices fresh **root ginger**, peeled and finely chopped

75 g (3 oz) **bamboo shoots**, finely chopped

1 **egg white**, lightly beaten

1 tablespoon **shoyu sauce** or **tamari sauce**

½ teaspoon **pepper**

1 teaspoon **Chinese rice wine** or **dry sherry**

1 teaspoon **sesame oil**

1 teaspoon **cornflour**

20 PREP

10 COOK

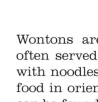
6 SERVES

party

Wonton soup

Wontons are small dumplings, which are often served in soup either on their own or with noodles. They are a very popular street food in oriental countries. Wonton wrappers can be found in the chiller cabinet in Chinese supermarkets and can be frozen, ideally on the day they are bought.

1 Make the stuffing. In a large bowl, mix all the ingredients together.

2 Put about ½ teaspoon of the stuffing in the centre of each wonton wrapper. Brush 2 of the edges of each wrapper with water, fold over the filling and seal to make a triangle.

3 Bring a large saucepan of water to the boil. Meanwhile, heat the stock in a separate saucepan and add the Chinese leaves.

4 Gently lower a handful of wontons into the boiling water with a slotted spoon. Stir very gently to separate the wontons and to make sure that they don't stick to the pan bottom.

5 Return the water to the boil and cook the wontons for 5–6 minutes or until they have floated to the surface. Using a slotted spoon, transfer them to a large serving bowl.

6 Pour the stock and Chinese leaves over the wontons and serve immediately, sprinkled with the spring onions.

Tofu in lemon grass fragrant broth

This low-fat yet flavourful soup is very easy to prepare and makes an excellent starter for a vegetarian meal.

PREP **15**

COOK **30**

SERVES **4**

fresh

1 Put the stock in a large, heavy-based saucepan and bring to the boil. Add the lemon grass and red chilli. Reduce the heat, cover and simmer for 15–20 minutes.

2 Add the shoyu or tamari sauce and pepper, then stir in the mushrooms and tofu. Simmer for 5–10 minutes.

3 Add the lime juice, basil leaves and spring onions and stir gently. Serve immediately.

1 litre (1¾ pints) **Vegetable Stock** (see page 19)

2 **lemon grass stalks**, lightly crushed

1 **red chilli**, chopped

2 teaspoons **shoyu sauce** or **tamari sauce**

pinch of **white pepper**

200 g (7 oz) **closed-cap mushrooms**, chopped

250 g (8 oz) **firm tofu**, cut into cubes

juice of ½ **lime**

handful of **basil** leaves

2 **spring onions**, sliced lengthways

250 g (8 oz) dried **udon noodles**

150 g (5 oz) firm **tofu**, diced

25 g (1 oz) dried **wakame seaweed**

4 **spring onions**, thinly sliced

1.5 litres (2½ pints) **Vegetable Stock** (see page 19)

3 tablespoons **miso paste**

2 tablespoons **dark soy sauce**

2 tablespoons **mirin**

15

PREP

7

COOK

4

SERVES

light

Japanese miso soup with noodles

This light, healthy soup has a rich flavour. Miso, made from fermented soy bean paste, is a classic ingredient in Japanese cooking, as is wakame seaweed and mirin. Look out for miso and wakame in health food stores and larger supermarkets, and mirin in larger supermarkets and Asian food stores.

1 Cook the udon noodles in a saucepan of boiling water for 4 minutes. Drain well and transfer to warm soup bowls. Top with the tofu, wakame and spring onions.

2 Meanwhile, put the stock, miso paste, soy sauce and mirin in a large, heavy-based saucepan and bring to the boil. Reduce the heat and simmer gently for 3–4 minutes. Pour into the bowls and serve immediately.

Noodle soup with enoki mushrooms

This big-bowl Japanese soup contains just about everything for one meal. Tofu goes well with other oriental ingredients, but you can use prawns or grilled chicken fillets instead. The strange-looking enoki mushrooms are available in large supermarkets, but if hard to find, use fresh shiitake mushrooms.

1 Heat the oil in a large, nonstick frying pan, add the tofu and cook until crisp and golden brown on all sides. Remove with a slotted spoon and drain on kitchen paper.

2 Meanwhile, put the stock in a large, heavy-based saucepan and bring to the boil. Reduce the heat, add the vinegar, mirin and onion and simmer gently for 2 minutes.

3 Cook the udon or egg noodles in a saucepan of boiling water for 1 minute. Drain well and transfer to warm soup bowls. Add the bean sprouts, chilli and spring onions.

4 Add the mushrooms to the stock and cook for 1 minute. Remove with a slotted spoon and arrange on top of the noodles with the fried tofu. Sprinkle with the fried garlic and coriander leaves.

5 Stir the miso paste and lime leaves into the stock. Ladle the stock over the ingredients in the bowls and serve piping hot. Serve the soup accompanied with side dishes of soy sauce and chilli flakes.

15

PREP

6

COOK

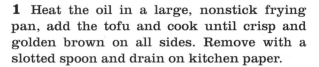

4

SERVES

stylish

4 tablespoons **vegetable oil**

250 g (8 oz) firm **tofu**, cut into cubes

1.2 litres (2 pints) **Vegetable Stock** (see page 19)

1 tablespoon **rice wine vinegar**

1 tablespoon **mirin**

1 **sweet white onion**, sliced

250 g (8 oz) fresh **udon noodles** or **egg noodles**

125 g (4 oz) **bean sprouts**

1 **red chilli**, thinly sliced

4 **spring onions**, thinly sliced

50 g (2 oz) **enoki mushrooms**

1 tablespoon **fried garlic**

handful of fresh **coriander**

2 tablespoons **miso paste**

4 **kaffir lime leaves**, shredded

TO GARNISH:

light soy sauce

dried **chilli flakes**

chilled

50 g (2 oz) **bread**

125 g (4 oz) **raisins**

125 g (4 oz) **blanched almonds**, toasted

3 tablespoons **olive oil**

3 **garlic cloves**, crushed or roughly chopped

900 ml (1½ pints) **milk** or **water**

hyssop flowers or **borage flowers**, to garnish

15*

PREP

COOK

6

SERVES

party

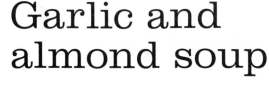

Garlic and almond soup

This soup is quite rich and should be served in small quantities. Known in ancient Rome, it has always been considered beneficial to good health, with its antibacterial and heart-protecting properties.

1 Roughly tear the bread into small pieces and put them in a small bowl. Put the raisins in a separate bowl and cover both the bread and raisins with water. Leave to soak for 30–60 minutes or until the raisins are plump.

2 Remove the bread from the water and squeeze to remove the excess moisture. In a blender or food processor, blend the bread with the almonds to form a smooth paste.

3 Add the oil, garlic, raisins and milk or water and blend again until smooth.

4 Cover the soup and chill in the refrigerator for 2–3 hours to allow the flavours to mingle. Serve in small soup bowls topped with hyssop or borage flowers.

* Plus 2½–4 hours soaking and chilling

Vichyssoise

15 *
PREP

40
COOK

6
SERVES

classic

This well-known French-sounding soup was actually created in the USA, and although the name is usually used for chilled leek and potato soups thickened with cream, the basic recipe can be successfully adapted to other vegetables, such as courgettes.

1 Slice off the green tops of the leeks and set aside for use in another recipe. Slice the white parts of the leeks thinly.

2 Melt the butter in a large, heavy-based saucepan, add the leeks and onion and cook over a moderate heat for 5 minutes or until softened but not coloured.

3 Add the stock, nutmeg and potatoes and season to taste with salt and pepper. Bring to the boil. Reduce the heat, partially cover the pan and simmer for 25 minutes. Pour in the milk and simmer for a further 5–8 minutes. Leave to cool slightly.

4 In a blender or food processor, blend the soup in batches until smooth, then rub it through a sieve into a bowl. Add the single cream, stir well and cover closely. Chill in the refrigerator for at least 3 hours. Just before serving, swirl in the double cream. Taste and adjust the seasoning if necessary. Serve in chilled bowls, garnishing each portion with a generous sprinkling of snipped chives.

1 kg (2 lb) **leeks**

50 g (2 oz) **butter**

1 **onion**, chopped

1 litre (1¾ pints) **Vegetable Stock** (see page 19)

pinch of **grated nutmeg**

750 g (1½ lb) old **potatoes**, diced

600 ml (1 pint) **milk**

300 ml (½ pint) **single cream**

150 ml (¼ pint) **double cream**, chilled

salt and **white pepper**

2 tablespoons snipped **chives**, to garnish

* Plus 3 hours chilling

50 g (2 oz) **butter**

1 **onion**, chopped

500 g (1 lb) **carrots**, sliced

375 g (12 oz) **leeks**, white parts only, sliced

600 ml (1 pint) **water**

600 ml (1 pint) **Vegetable Stock** (see page 19)

1 teaspoon chopped fresh **coriander**

150 ml (¼ pint) **double cream**, chilled

salt and **pepper**

finely chopped **parsley** or fresh **coriander**, to garnish

15*

PREP

45

COOK

6

SERVES

stylish

Carrot vichyssoise

Winter vegetables are used in this version of the traditional Vichyssoise, which is finished with fresh herbs. To chill the bowls, simply place them in the refrigerator with the soup.

1 Melt the butter in a large, heavy-based saucepan, add the onion and cook over a moderate heat for 5 minutes or until softened but not coloured. Add the carrots and leeks and cook, stirring, for 2–3 minutes. Add, the measured water, stock and coriander. Season to taste with salt.

2 Bring to the boil, then reduce the heat, cover and simmer for 30–35 minutes until the vegetables are tender. Leave to cool slightly.

3 In a blender or food processor, blend the soup in batches until smooth, then transfer it to a bowl. Cover closely. Chill in the refrigerator for at least 3 hours. Just before serving, stir in the chilled cream. Serve in chilled soup bowls and sprinkle each portion with finely chopped parsley or coriander to garnish.

* Plus 3 hours chilling

Prawn vichyssoise

Prawns work well in chilled soups because they taste equally good hot or cold. You could add a couple of cooked, unpeeled prawns to the side of each bowl.

1 Slice off the green tops of the leeks and set aside for use in another recipe. Slice the white parts of the leeks thinly.

2 Melt the butter in a large, heavy-based saucepan, add the leeks and onion and cook over a moderate heat for 5 minutes or until softened but not coloured.

3 Add the stock, nutmeg and potatoes and season to taste with salt and pepper. Bring to the boil. Reduce the heat, partially cover and simmer for 25 minutes. Pour in the milk and simmer for a further 5–8 minutes. Leave to cool slightly.

4 In a blender or food processor, blend the soup in batches until smooth, then rub it through a sieve into a bowl. Add the single cream and prawns, stir well and cover closely. Chill in the refrigerator for at least 3 hours. Just before serving, swirl in the double cream. Taste and adjust the seasoning if necessary. Serve in chilled bowls, garnishing each portion with a few extra prawns.

15* PREP

40 COOK

6 SERVES

rich

1 kg (2 lb) **leeks**

50 g (2 oz) **butter**

1 **onion**, chopped

1 litre (1¾ pints) **Vegetable Stock** (see page 19)

pinch of **grated nutmeg**

750 g (1½ lb) old **potatoes**, diced

600 ml (1 pint) **milk**

300 ml (½ pint) **single cream**

175 g (6 oz) cooked peeled **prawns**, plus extra to garnish

150 ml (¼ pint) **double cream**, chilled

salt and **white pepper**

* Plus 3 hours chilling

4 slices of day-old **bread**, crusts removed

125 g (4 oz) **blanched almonds**, roughly chopped

1–2 **garlic cloves**, chopped

100 ml (3½ fl oz) extra virgin **olive oil**

2–3 tablespoons **sherry vinegar**

1 litre (1¾ pints) iced **water**

salt

250 g (8 oz) **white seedless grapes**, to garnish

15*

PREP

COOK

4

SERVES

light

White gazpacho

Bread and almonds form the basis of this creamy coloured soup, which is based on the Spanish original. The consistency should be thin, as this is a light summer dish.

1 Put the bread in a bowl, cover with cold water and leave to soak for 5 minutes. Remove from the water and squeeze to remove the excess moisture.

2 In a blender or food processor, blend the the almonds and garlic until very finely ground and almost paste-like. With the motor running, gradually add the bread and blend until smooth, then gradually add the oil in a thin, steady stream. When the oil has been incorporated, add the vinegar, scraping down the sides of the bowl if necessary. Pour in 300 ml (½ pint) of the measured iced water and blend briefly to combine.

3 Strain through a sieve into a large bowl, pressing with the back of a ladle to extract as much liquid as possible. Stir in the remaining iced water to make a thin soup. Season to taste with salt. Cover closely and chill in the refrigerator for at least 3 hours.

4 Just before serving, stir the soup well. Ladle into individual chilled bowls and serve garnished with a few grapes.

* Plus 3 hours chilling

Beetroot gazpacho

15[*]

PREP

COOK

This stunning, deep-pink soup is even better if it's allowed to infuse and chill for an hour before serving. It makes a perfect no-fuss appetizer for entertaining because you can prepare it in advance and simply serve it when you and your guests are ready to eat.

4

SERVES

1 In a blender or food processor, blend the beetroot, onion, garlic, tomatoes, capers and cornichons until smooth.

2 Add the breadcrumbs and blend, then gradually blend in the stock, oil and vinegar to form a smooth soup. Season to taste with salt and pepper.

3 Serve the soup in chilled soup bowls, topped with a spoonful of crème fraîche and some chopped dill, and sprinkled with pepper.

easy

500 g (1 lb) cooked **beetroot in natural juices**, drained and chopped

1 small **onion**, roughly chopped

2 **garlic cloves**, roughly chopped

2 **tomatoes**, roughly chopped

2 tablespoons **capers**, drained

4 baby **cornichons**, drained and chopped

25 g (1 oz) dry **breadcrumbs**

600 ml (1 pint) **Vegetable Stock** (see page 19)

150 ml (¼ pint) extra virgin **olive oil**

2 tablespoons **white wine vinegar**

salt and **pepper**

TO SERVE:

crème fraîche

chopped **dill**

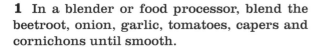

* Plus 3 hours chilling

1 **red pepper**, cored, deseeded and roughly chopped

1 **green pepper**, cored, deseeded and roughly chopped

1.5 kg (3 lb) **tomatoes**, skinned and roughly chopped

2 **garlic cloves**, crushed

1 slice of day-old **bread**, crusts removed

5 tablespoons **olive oil**

6 tablespoons **white wine vinegar**

1 teaspoon golden **caster sugar**

6 tablespoons **water**

6–8 **ice cubes**, plus extra to serve

TO SERVE:

1 **red pepper**, cored, deseeded and finely diced

1 **green pepper**, cored, deseeded and finely diced

1 small **cucumber**, finely diced

1 **red onion**, finely diced

flat leaf parsley leaves

20*

PREP

COOK

Gazpacho with raw salsa

This colourful and wonderfully refreshing soup, made with sweet peppers and tomatoes, is packed with flavour and vitality.

6

SERVES

fresh

1 In a blender or food processor, blend the red and green peppers, tomatoes and garlic to form a fairly smooth purée.

2 Roughly tear the bread into small pieces and add to the tomato mixture with the oil, vinegar and sugar. Add the measured water and blend until smooth. Add the ice cubes, then cover and chill in the refrigerator for at least 1 hour.

3 Serve the chilled soup with extra ice cubes and topped with the diced peppers, cucumber, red onion and parsley leaves.

* Plus 1 hour chilling

Gazpacho and almond soup

Gazpacho is the classic cold vegetable soup of Spain, with as many different recipes as there are towns. This version is thickened with almonds, but you could use dry or fresh breadcrumbs instead. Reserve some of the diced vegetables to garnish.

1 Remove the cores from the tomatoes with a small, sharp knife. Plunge them into boiling water for 5–10 seconds, then remove and refresh in cold water. Slip off the skins and discard. Cut in half around the centre and gently squeeze out and discard the seeds. Dice the flesh.

2 In a blender or food processor, blend the diced tomatoes, onion, garlic, peppers, cucumber, chillies, olives and capers until fairly smooth. Add the ground almonds and blend again to thicken.

3 Transfer the mixture to a bowl and stir in the vinegar, sugar, cold stock, tomato juice and oil. Cover and chill in the refrigerator for at least 1 hour, then stir in the herbs. Season to taste with salt and pepper. Serve in chilled soup bowls.

25*
PREP

COOK

6
SERVES

tasty

1 kg (2 lb) vine-ripened **tomatoes**

1 **red onion**, chopped

4 **garlic cloves**

2 **green peppers** or **red peppers**, cored, deseeded and chopped

½ **cucumber**, peeled and chopped

2 **red chillies**, deseeded and chopped

25 g (1 oz) pitted **green olives**, chopped

1 tablespoon **capers**

50 g (2 oz) **ground almonds**, toasted

3 tablespoons **red wine vinegar**

1 tablespoon **sugar**

450 ml (¾ pint) cold **Vegetable Stock** (see page 19)

150 ml (¼ pint) **tomato juice**

150 ml (¼ pint) extra virgin **olive oil**

2 tablespoons chopped **parsley**

2 tablespoons chopped fresh **coriander**

salt and **pepper**

* Plus 1 hour chilling

1 small **red onion**, chopped

2 **garlic cloves**, chopped

2.5 cm (1 inch) piece of fresh **root ginger**, peeled and grated

1 small **red pepper**, cored, deseeded and chopped

2 **red chillies**, deseeded and chopped

500 g (1 lb) ripe **tomatoes**, chopped

2 tablespoons chopped fresh **coriander**

4 **poppadums**, crumbled

300 ml (½ pint) cold **Vegetable Stock** (see page 19)

300 ml (½ pint) **tomato juice**

4 tablespoons extra virgin **olive oil**

2 tablespoons **white wine vinegar**

salt and **pepper**

TO GARNISH:

natural yogurt

poppadums

sprigs of fresh **coriander**

20* PREP

COOK

4

SERVES

spicy

Gazpacho with Indian flavours

A classic Spanish gazpacho is given an exotic twist with the addition of Indian spices and poppadums to make a refreshing soup for a hot summer's day.

1 In a blender or food processor, blend the onion, garlic, ginger, red pepper, chillies, tomatoes, coriander and crumbled poppadums until smooth.

2 Transfer the mixture to a bowl and stir in the remaining ingredients. Season to taste with salt and pepper. Cover closely and freeze for at least **15 minutes** until well chilled.

3 Spoon the gazpacho into chilled soup bowls and serve garnished with yogurt, poppadums and coriander sprigs.

* Plus 15 minutes freezing

Chilled borscht with apple

15* PREP

40 COOK

4 SERVES

stylish

500 g (1 lb) raw **beetroot**

1 small **fennel bulb**

600 ml (1 pint) **water**

600 ml (1 pint) **apple juice**

1 teaspoon **thyme leaves**

4 tablespoons **lemon juice**

1 tablespoon snipped **chives**

salt and **pepper**

soda bread, to serve

Beetroot has an amazing colour and is packed with iron, beta-carotene and folic acid. Here it teams well with apple in an adaptation of the traditional Russian soup. You can add chilled soured cream or a spoonful of natural yogurt just before serving.

1 Peel the beetroot and cut the flesh into thin matchstick strips.

2 Trim the fennel and cut the bulb into strips. Put the beetroot and fennel in a large, heavy-based saucepan with the measured water and bring slowly to the boil. Reduce the heat, cover and simmer gently for 20–30 minutes or until the vegetables are tender.

3 Add the apple juice and thyme leaves and season to taste with salt and pepper. Simmer for a further 10 minutes. Remove from the heat and stir in the lemon juice and chives. Taste and adjust the seasoning if necessary.

4 Leave the soup to cool, then pour it into a bowl, cover closely and chill in the refrigerator for at least 3 hours. Ladle into chilled bowls and serve with soda bread.

* Plus 3 hours chilling

2 **onions**, chopped

2 **carrots**, chopped

3 sprigs of **parsley**

6 **black peppercorns**

1 **bay leaf**

1 litre (1¾ pints) **water**

4 cooked peeled **beetroot**, grated

1 **sugar cube** or
1 teaspoon **caster sugar**

2 teaspoons **white wine vinegar**

1½ teaspoons **powdered gelatine**

salt

TO GARNISH:

150 ml (¼ pint) **soured cream**

1 teaspoon mild **curry powder**

snipped **chives**

20*

PREP

90

COOK

4

SERVES

fresh

Chilled beetroot soup

Beetroot's distinctive red juice is something to be wary of when preparing the vegetable, as it readily stains. So take care to protect both your hands and clothes.

1 Put the onions, carrots, parsley, peppercorns and bay leaf in a large, heavy-based saucepan, add the measured water and bring to the boil. Reduce the heat, cover and simmer for 1 hour or until the vegetables are tender.

2 Strain the stock through a sieve into the bowl containing the beetroot and mix well, discarding the solids in the sieve. Transfer the beetroot and stock to a clean saucepan and add the sugar and vinegar. Season to taste with salt. Simmer gently for 10 minutes without boiling. Strain into a clean saucepan, discarding the beetroot.

3 Spoon 2 tablespoons of the hot soup into a cup or jug. Add the gelatine and stir until thoroughly dissolved. Stir the mixture into the pan. Leave to cool, then pour into a bowl, cover closely and chill in the refrigerator for at least 3 hours or until set.

4 In a small bowl, mix the soured cream with the curry powder. Break up the soup and serve in chilled bowls, garnished with the soured cream mixture and snipped chives.

* Plus 3 hours
chilling

Iced tomato soup with salsa verde

This soup relies on full-flavoured, sun-ripened tomatoes to conjure up the taste of southern Italy. Adding the salsa verde gives the soup a sweet and sour flavour, popular in the south of Italy and Sicily. The salsa will keep for up to a week in the refrigerator.

25* PREP

COOK

6 SERVES

party

1 Remove the cores from the tomatoes with a small, sharp knife. Plunge them into boiling water for 5–10 seconds, then remove and refresh in cold water. Slip off the skins and discard. Cut in half around the centre and gently squeeze out and discard the seeds.

2 Core and deseed the red peppers, then roughly chop. Deseed the chilli and finely chop. In a blender or food processor, blend the tomatoes, chilli and garlic to a rough purée. Transfer to a bowl and stir in the passata, oil and vinegar. Season to taste with salt and pepper. Cover closely and chill overnight.

3 Meanwhile, make the salsa verde. Put 1 teaspoon salt and the garlic in a mortar and pound with a pestle until creamy. Transfer to a bowl and stir in the anchovies, herbs, capers, oil and lemon juice. Season to taste with pepper. Transfer to a jar and pour a layer of oil on top to exclude the air.

4 Stir the crushed ice into the soup and serve in chilled soup bowls, with the salsa verde separately in a bowl to stir into the soup.

* Plus overnight chilling

1 kg (2 lb) vine-ripened **tomatoes**

2 large **red peppers**

1 small **red chilli**

2 **garlic cloves**, chopped

600 ml (1 pint) **passata**

6 tablespoons extra virgin **olive oil**

2 tablespoons **balsamic vinegar** (or to taste)

salt and **pepper**

600 ml (1 pint) **crushed ice**, to serve

SALSA VERDE:

2 **garlic cloves**, finely chopped

4 **anchovy fillets** in oil, rinsed and chopped

3 tablespoons chopped **parsley**

3 tablespoons chopped **mint**

3 tablespoons chopped **basil**

2 tablespoons **capers**

150 ml (¼ pint) extra virgin **olive oil**, plus extra to seal

2 tablespoons **lemon juice**

25 g (1 oz) **butter**

2 tablespoons **olive oil**

1 large **onion**, chopped

1 **garlic clove**, chopped

about 1 kg (2 lb) **tomatoes**, skinned and roughly chopped

900 ml (1½ pints) **Chicken Stock** (see page 17)

1 teaspoon chopped **oregano**

1½ teaspoons **caster sugar**

¼ teaspoon **celery salt**

pinch of **grated nutmeg**

1 tablespoon **Worcestershire sauce**

150 ml (¼ pint) **soured cream**

salt and **pepper**

TO GARNISH:

6 **Spanish olives**, pitted

chopped **parsley**

20* PREP

55 COOK

6 SERVES

classic

Chilled tomato soup

This light, tasty soup is an ideal starter for a summer lunch. Replace the chicken stock with homemade vegetable stock if you are cooking for vegetarians.

1 Melt the butter with the oil in a large, heavy-based saucepan, add the onion and garlic and cook over a moderate heat for 5 minutes or until softened but not coloured. Add the tomatoes and cook, stirring, for 3 minutes.

2 Add the stock, oregano, sugar, celery salt, nutmeg and Worcestershire sauce. Season to taste with salt and pepper. Stir well and bring to the boil, then reduce the heat, partially cover and simmer for 45 minutes. Leave to cool slightly.

3 In a blender or food processor, blend the soup in batches, then transfer it to a bowl. Stir in the soured cream and leave the soup to cool completely. Cover the bowl closely and chill in the refrigerator for at least 3 hours.

4 Meanwhile, put an olive in each section of a 6-cube ice-cube tray and top with cold water. Freeze until solid. Serve the soup in chilled bowls, each portion garnished with an olive ice cube and a sprinkling of chopped parsley.

* Plus 3 hours chilling

Chilled yogurt, cucumber and mint soup

Cool and refreshing yogurt soup, spiced with cumin and chilli, makes a gentle start to a spicy Indian meal. It has a slightly sharp, piquant flavour, and the addition of finely chopped cucumber and tomato gives it a lovely bite.

1 In a blender or food processor, blend the yogurt, stock, ginger, cumin and chilli powder until smooth. Transfer to a bowl.

2 Add the cucumber, tomatoes and mint to the yogurt mixture. Season to taste with salt and pepper and stir to combine.

3 Cover closely and chill in the refrigerator for 30 minutes. To serve, ladle the soup into chilled bowls, drizzle over a little extra yogurt and sprinkle over some roasted cumin seeds to garnish.

15*

PREP

COOK

4

SERVES

light

750 ml (1¼ pints) **natural yogurt**, plus extra to serve

750 ml (1¼ pints) **Vegetable Stock** (see page 19)

½ teaspoon finely grated fresh **ginger root**

½ teaspoon **ground cumin**

¼ teaspoon **chilli powder**

1 small **cucumber**, finely diced

2 **plum tomatoes**, deseeded and diced

4 tablespoons finely chopped **mint**

salt and **pepper**

roasted **cumin seeds**, to garnish

* Plus 30 minutes chilling

50 g (2 oz) **butter**

2 bunches of **watercress**, stalks discarded, roughly chopped, plus extra leaves to garnish

1 litre (1¾ pints) **Vegetable Stock** (see page 19)

250 g (8 oz) **potatoes**, chopped

pinch of **grated nutmeg**

salt and **pepper**

TO GARNISH:

150 ml (¼ pint) **single cream**, chilled

1 tablespoon **olive oil** (optional)

10*

PREP

25

COOK

4

SERVES

stylish

Chilled watercress soup

One of the great advantages of serving chilled soups is that they can be prepared in advance and kept in the refrigerator until you're ready to eat. And in addition, no reheating is required!

1 Melt the butter in a large, heavy-based saucepan, add the watercress and cook over a moderate heat, stirring, for 3 minutes. Add the stock, potatoes and nutmeg. Season to taste with pepper. Bring to the boil, then reduce the heat, cover and simmer for 15–20 minutes or until the potatoes are tender. Leave to cool.

2 In a blender or food processor, blend the soup in batches until smooth, then transfer it to a large bowl. Cover closely and chill in the refrigerator for at least 3 hours.

3 Just before serving, fold in the chilled cream. Taste and add salt if necessary. Serve in chilled bowls, garnishing each portion with a few watercress leaves, pepper and a drizzle of olive oil, if liked.

* Plus 3 hours chilling

Chilled lettuce and dill soup

PREP
10*

COOK
25

Dill is a delicate herb with a distinctive flavour, and it's perfect for this summer soup. The light, fresh taste of the lettuce makes this ideal for alfresco eating.

SERVES
4

herby

1 Melt the butter in a large, heavy-based saucepan, add the onion and cook over a moderate heat for about 5 minutes or until softened. Add the flour and cook, stirring constantly, for 2 minutes. Whisk in the stock and bring to the boil, whisking constantly.

2 Add the lettuce, 2 tablespoons of the dill and the nutmeg. Reduce the heat, cover and simmer, stirring occasionally, for about 15 minutes. Leave to cool.

3 In a blender or food processor, blend the soup in batches, then transfer it to a bowl. Stir in the lemon juice and pepper, and season to taste with salt. Cover closely and chill in the refrigerator for at least 3 hours.

4 In a small bowl, mix the remaining dill with the cream. Serve the soup in chilled bowls, garnishing each portion with a swirl of the cream and dill mixture.

50 g (2 oz) **butter**

1 small **onion**, chopped

1 tablespoon **plain flour**

900 ml (1½ pints) **Vegetable Stock** (see page 19)

outer leaves of 2 **round lettuces**, roughly shredded

3 tablespoons chopped **dill**

pinch of **grated nutmeg**

1 tablespoon **lemon juice**

¼–½ teaspoon **white pepper**

salt

4 tablespoons **double cream**, to garnish

* Plus 3 hours chilling

5 **potatoes**, diced

3 **onions**, sliced

475 g (15 oz) can **cream of mushroom soup**

25 g (1 oz) **butter**

900 ml (1½ pints) **milk**

1 teaspoon prepared **English mustard**

salt and **pepper**

TO GARNISH:

2 tablespoons **cottage cheese**

few snipped **chives**

paprika

PREP
10*

COOK
20

SERVES
6

filling

Chilled potato chowder

We tend to think of chowders as being winter soups, but this recipe proves that they taste just as good when chilled. The soup is rubbed through a sieve rather then being blended so that it retains a pleasantly coarse texture.

1 Put the potatoes and onions in a large saucepan, add just enough water to cover and bring to the boil. Reduce the heat and simmer for 15 minutes, or until tender. Drain and rub the mixture through a coarse sieve into a clean saucepan.

2 Add the soup, butter, milk and mustard. Season to taste with salt and pepper and stir to mix. Heat gently until the soup begins to simmer. Pour into a bowl and leave to cool. Cover closely and chill in the refrigerator for at least 3 hours.

3 Serve the soup in chilled bowls, garnishing each portion with a little cottage cheese, a few snipped chives and a dusting of paprika.

* Plus 3 hours chilling

Chilled avocado soup

10*

PREP

COOK

4

SERVES

quick

This delicately flavoured, easy-to-prepare soup must not be left for longer than 1 hour before it is served or it will lose its pale green colour. Make sure that all the ingredients are well chilled.

1 Cut the avocados in half and remove and discard the stones. Peel the flesh and slice it into a blender or food processor, discarding any discoloured flesh.

2 Add the lemon juice, yogurt and 600 ml (1 pint) of the stock and blend the mixture to a smooth purée. Transfer to a bowl.

3 Whisk in the chilled cream, then add the remaining stock, cayenne pepper and pepper. Season to taste with salt. Stir well, cover closely and chill in the refrigerator for 1 hour.

4 Serve the soup in chilled bowls, sprinkling each portion with snipped chives to garnish.

2 large ripe **avocados**

1 teaspoon **lemon juice**

150 ml (¼ pint) **natural yogurt**

750 ml (1¼ pints) **Chicken Stock** (see page 17), chilled

4 tablespoons **single cream**, chilled

cayenne pepper

¼ teaspoon **white pepper**

salt

2 tablespoons snipped **chives**, to garnish

* Plus 1 hour chilling

250 g (8 oz) **celery**

1.2 litres (2 pints) **Vegetable Stock** (see page 19)

1 **onion**, chopped

250 g (8 oz) **potatoes**, diced

1 teaspoon **ground cumin**

3 tablespoons chilled **soured cream**

salt

finely chopped **celery leaves**, to garnish

15 *

PREP

25

COOK

4

SERVES

simple

Chilled celery soup with cumin

An unusual combination! The cumin gives a touch of aromatic flavour to the subtle taste of the celery.

1 Thinly slice enough celery to yield 2 tablespoons. Set aside in a small bowl. Grate the remaining celery.

2 Combine the grated celery, stock, onion, potatoes and cumin in a large, heavy-based saucepan. Season to taste with salt. Bring to the boil, then reduce the heat, partially cover and cook for 20–25 minutes.

3 In a blender or food processor, blend the soup in batches until smooth, then transfer it to a bowl. Add the reserved sliced celery and stir well. Leave to cool. Cover closely and chill in the refrigerator for at least 3 hours.

4 Just before serving, stir in the soured cream. Serve in chilled bowls, garnished with finely chopped celery leaves.

* Plus 3 hours chilling

Chilled courgette soup

15[*]

PREP

This is the perfect soup for a light lunch. Courgettes and potatoes are flavoured with fresh ginger and a hint of nutmeg. A dash of cream finishes the dish.

55

COOK

1 Cut off the ends of the courgettes and slice thickly into a colander. Sprinkle with salt and leave to drain for 10–15 minutes. Rinse under cold running water, drain thoroughly and pat dry with kitchen paper.

2 Melt the butter in a large, heavy-based saucepan, add the onions and cook over a moderate heat for 5 minutes or until softened but not coloured. Add the courgettes and cook over a low heat, stirring frequently, for 5 minutes.

3 Add the stock, ginger and nutmeg. Season to taste with pepper. Bring to the boil and add the potatoes. Reduce the heat, partially cover and simmer for 40–45 minutes or until the vegetables are very tender.

4 In a blender or food processor, blend the soup in batches until smooth, then transfer it to a bowl. Leave to cool, then cover closely and chill in the refrigerator for at least 3 hours.

5 Serve in chilled bowls, garnishing each portion with a swirl of chilled cream.

6

SERVES

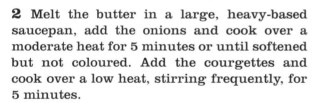

thick

1.5 kg (3 lb) small **courgettes**

50 g (2 oz) **butter**

250 g (8 oz) **onions**, chopped

1 litre (1¾ pints) **Vegetable Stock** (see page 19)

1 tablespoon grated fresh **root ginger**

pinch of **grated nutmeg**

375 g (12 oz) **potatoes**, diced

salt and **pepper**

150 ml (¼ pint) **single cream**, chilled, to garnish

* Plus 10–15 minutes draining and 3 hours chilling

50 g (2 oz) **butter**

1 small **onion**, chopped

500 g (1 lb) frozen **peas**

¼ teaspoon **caster sugar**

1.2 litres (2 pints)
Vegetable Stock
(see page 19)

4 tablespoons chopped
mint

300 g (10 oz) **potatoes**,
roughly chopped

150 ml (¼ pint) **double
cream**

salt and **white pepper**

10*

PREP

35

COOK

6

SERVES

herby

Chilled pea soup with mint

Peas and mint are the perfect match for a summer soup, and this chilled version of a classic soup is wonderfully refreshing. You can use freshly podded peas if you prefer.

1 Melt the butter in a large, heavy-based saucepan, add the onion and cook over a moderate heat for 5 minutes or until softened but not coloured.

2 Add the peas, sugar, stock and 3 table-spoons of the mint. Season to taste with pepper. Stir well and bring to the boil. Add the potatoes, then reduce the heat, partially cover and simmer for 20–25 minutes.

3 In a blender or food processor, blend the soup in batches until smooth, then transfer it to a clean saucepan. Taste and adjust the seasoning if necessary, add the cream and stir well. Heat gently without boiling. Leave to cool, then cover closely and chill in the refrigerator for at least 3 hours.

4 Serve in chilled bowls, garnishing each portion with some of the remaining chopped mint.

* Plus 3 hours
chilling

Chilled cucumber and pepper soup

This impressive-looking soup uses crunchy pepper and cucumber as a garnish. If you're preparing the soup in advance, wait until you're ready to serve before preparing the garnish ingredients because they should be as fresh as possible.

30* PREP

15 COOK

4 SERVES

party

1 Cut one-third of one of the cucumbers into fine dice and reserve for the garnish. Chop the remaining cucumbers roughly.

2 In a blender or food processor, blend the chopped cucumber and garlic until very smooth. Pour into a bowl and mix with the yogurt. Add enough of the measured iced water to make a smooth soup. Season to taste with salt and pepper and stir in the mint. Cover and chill in the refrigerator for 4 hours.

3 Chop 1 yellow pepper into fine dice, mix with the reserved cucumber and set aside for the garnish. Chop the remaining pepper. Put in a small saucepan with the lime or lemon juice, sugar, measured water and cayenne pepper. Bring to the boil, then reduce the heat and simmer for 10–15 minutes until tender and the liquid has reduced. In a blender or food processor, blend until smooth. Strain through a sieve into a bowl. Leave to cool, cover and chill in the refrigerator for 4 hours.

4 Serve in bowls, sprinkled with the pepper and cucumber. Drizzle over the pepper purée.

2 **cucumbers**, peeled and deseeded

1 **garlic clove**, crushed

250 g (8 oz) **natural yogurt**, preferably Greek

about 125 ml (4 fl oz) iced **water**

4 tablespoons chopped **mint**

2 **yellow peppers**, cored and deseeded

2 tablespoons **lime juice** or **lemon juice**

1 tablespoon **caster sugar**

75 ml (3 fl oz) **water**

pinch of **cayenne pepper**

salt and **pepper**

* Plus 4 hours chilling

½ teaspoon **salt**

300 ml (½ pint) **water**

300 g (10 oz) **asparagus**

1 tablespoon **groundnut oil**

1 **garlic clove**, finely chopped

1 **shallot**, sliced

½ teaspoon crushed **dried chillies**

½ teaspoon **white pepper**

300 ml (½ pint) **coconut milk**

1 tablespoon **fish sauce** or **light soy sauce**

10*

PREP

20

COOK

4

SERVES

posh

Khun Tom's chilled asparagus

The coconut milk adds a touch of sweetness to this delicious asparagus soup, and dried chillies give the whole dish a lift. It's very quick and easy to prepare, but looks fantastic when served.

1 Put the salt and measured water in a large saucepan and bring to the boil. Add the asparagus and cook for 10–12 minutes until tender. Drain and reserve the water. Cut the tips off the asparagus and reserve for the garnish. In a blender or food processor, blend the remaining asparagus and its liquid until smooth. Set aside.

2 Heat the oil in a large, heavy-based saucepan, add the garlic, shallot, chillies and pepper and cook over a moderate heat, stirring, for 1 minute. Add the puréed asparagus. Bring to the boil and add the coconut milk. Boil for 2 minutes, then add the fish or soy sauce. Leave to cool, then cover and chill in the refrigerator for 4 hours.

3 Serve in chilled soup bowls, garnished with the reserved asparagus tips.

* Plus 4 hours chilling

Chilled spinach soup

The vibrant colour and rich, creamy flavour of this soup will make it an instant favourite. The soured cream makes it quite rich, so you only need a small amount of soup – perfect for a starter.

1 Melt the butter in a large, heavy-based saucepan, add the chopped onion and cook over a moderate heat for 5 minutes or until softened but not coloured. Add the spinach and cook, stirring constantly, until wilted.

2 Stir in the stock, potatoes, lemon juice, nutmeg and salt and pepper to taste. Bring to the boil, then reduce the heat, partially cover and simmer for 10–12 minutes or until the potatoes are tender.

3 In a blender or food processor, blend the soup in batches until smooth, transferring to a bowl. Leave to cool, then cover and chill in the refrigerator for at least 3 hours.

4 In a small bowl, blend the soured cream with the grated onion and cucumber. Serve the soup in chilled bowls, each portion topped with a little of the soured cream mixture.

15 *

PREP

20

COOK

4

SERVES

rich

50 g (2 oz) **butter**

1 **onion**, chopped

500 g (1 lb) fresh or frozen **spinach**

1.2 litres (2 pints) **Vegetable Stock** (see page 19)

250 g (8 oz) **potatoes**, thinly sliced

1 teaspoon **lemon juice**

pinch of **grated nutmeg**

salt and **white pepper**

TO GARNISH:

150 ml (¼ pint) **soured cream**

1 teaspoon finely grated **onion**

2 tablespoons peeled and diced **cucumber**

* Plus 3 hours chilling

1 large **cucumber**

150 ml (¼ pint) **natural yogurt**

150 ml (¼ pint) **soured cream**

125 ml (4 fl oz) **milk**

¼ teaspoon **caster sugar**

¼ teaspoon **white pepper**

¼ teaspoon **Tabasco sauce**

200 g (7 oz) cooked peeled **prawns**, thawed if frozen

1 tablespoon finely chopped **mint**

1 tablespoon snipped **chives**

1 tablespoon chopped **dill**

salt

TO GARNISH:

4 small sprigs of **mint**

paprika, for dusting

10***

PREP

COOK

4

SERVES

herby

Chilled prawn and yogurt soup

This tangy, refreshing soup relies on the addition of really fresh herbs for its fragrant flavour and attractive colour.

1 Peel the cucumber. Cut it in half, remove and discard the seeds, then cut all the flesh into small dice. Put it in a sieve or colander, sprinkle with salt and leave to drain for 20 minutes. Rinse under cold running water, then drain thoroughly and pat dry with kitchen paper.

2 In a blender or food processor, blend together the yogurt, soured cream, milk, sugar, pepper and Tabasco sauce. Pour into a bowl and season to taste with salt.

3 Stir in the prawns, mint, chives and dill, then add the cucumber. Mix well, cover closely and chill in the refrigerator for at least 2 hours.

4 Serve the soup in chilled bowls, each portion garnished with a mint sprig and a dusting of paprika.

* Plus 20 minutes draining and 2 hours chilling

Chilled prawn and pea soup

20* PREP

30 COOK

4 SERVES

stylish

The shells of the prawns are full of flavour, which is why they're used here to infuse the stock. You can serve the soup with crisp wholemeal toast for dunking.

1 Pod the peas if using fresh, reserving the pods. Peel the prawns, reserving the shells. Cover the prawns and refrigerate. Put the prawn shells and pea pods in a large, heavy-based saucepan with the onion, garlic and stock or water. Bring to the boil, then reduce the heat and simmer gently for 15 minutes.

2 Strain the liquid into a clean saucepan, add the peas and nutmeg and season to taste with salt and pepper. Return to the boil, then reduce the heat and simmer until the peas are tender. In a blender or food processor, blend the soup in batches until smooth.

3 Pour the soup into a bowl and taste and adjust the seasoning if necessary. Stir in the wine (if using), soured cream and lemon juice. Leave to cool, then cover and chill in the refrigerator for at least 2 hours.

4 Pour the soup into individual bowls and divide the prawns between them. Add an extra spoonful of soured cream and a little salmon roe, if liked, and sprinkle with chives.

250 g (8 oz) **peas**, thawed if frozen

250 g (8 oz) cooked small **prawns**, unpeeled

1 **onion**, chopped

1 **garlic clove**, crushed

600 ml (1 pint) **Chicken Stock** (see page 17) or **water**

pinch of **grated nutmeg**

150 ml (¼ pint) **dry white wine** (optional)

150 ml (¼ pint) **soured cream**, plus extra to serve (optional)

1 tablespoon **lemon juice**

salt and **pepper**

TO SERVE:

4 teaspoons **salmon roe** (optional)

2 tablespoons snipped **chives**

* Plus 2 hours chilling

50 g (2 oz) **butter**

1 **onion**, chopped

1 **garlic clove**, finely chopped

250 g (8 oz) **smoked salmon**, finely chopped

3 tablespoons **plain flour**

900 ml (1½ pints) **Chicken Stock** (see page 17)

1 tablespoon **lemon juice**

1 **bay leaf**

¼ teaspoon **paprika**

150 ml (¼ pint) **single cream**

125 g (4 oz) cooked peeled **prawns**, thawed if frozen

1 teaspoon **dill**, chopped

salt and **white pepper**

6 sprigs of **dill**, to garnish

15*

PREP

20

COOK

6

SERVES

posh

Chilled cream of smoked salmon soup

Dill goes well with smoked salmon, and the addition of lemon juice adds a piquant edge to this sophisticated recipe.

1 Melt the butter in a large, heavy-based saucepan, add the onion and garlic and cook over a moderate heat for 1 minute. Add the salmon and cook, stirring, for 1 minute. Sprinkle over the flour and cook, stirring constantly, for 30 seconds. Gradually pour in the stock, stirring constantly. Bring to the boil, stirring constantly. Reduce the heat and simmer for 5 minutes.

2 Add the lemon juice, bay leaf and paprika. Season to taste with salt and pepper. Simmer for 5–8 minutes. Remove from the heat and leave to cool. Remove and discard the bay leaf.

3 In a blender or food processor, blend the soup in batches until smooth. Strain through a coarse sieve into a bowl. Stir in the cream, prawns and chopped dill. Leave to cool, then cover closely and chill in the refrigerator for 3–4 hours or overnight.

4 Serve the soup in chilled bowls, garnishing each portion with a dill sprig.

* Plus 3–4 hours or overnight chilling

Melon and Parma ham soup

A favourite Italian starter is transformed into a soup in this quick and simple recipe. The key is to use good-quality ingredients. Serve in wine glasses if you're entertaining.

10

PREP

COOK

1 Cut the melon in half and remove and discard the seeds.

2 In a blender or food processor, blend the melon flesh until smooth. Season to taste with salt and pepper.

3 Finely dice 4 of the ham slices and stir into the soup. Cut the remaining 4 ham slices into thin ribbons.

4 Serve the soup in chilled bowls, garnished with the ham ribbons and torn basil leaves.

4

SERVES

party

1 ripe **cantaloupe melon** or **charentais melon**, about 1.5 kg (3 lb)

8 slices of **Parma ham**

salt and **pepper**

red basil leaves, torn, to garnish

index

Executive Editor Nicky Hill

Editor Charlotte Macey

Executive Art Editor
Darren Southern

Designer Ginny Zeal

Senior Production Controller
Manjit Sihra